THE WORLD OF THE GULL

LIVING WORLD BOOKS

John K. Terres, Editor

The World of the
Gull

Text and Photographs by

David F. Costello

J. B. LIPPINCOTT COMPANY

Philadelphia and New York

59.3
C84w

Frontispiece: a herring gull rises from the sea. (Photo by Dorothy B. Taylor)

Contents

THE WORLD OF THE GULL

Meet the Gull

THE WORLD of the gull is almost the world itself. If you are watchful in your outdoor ramblings, at one time or another you can see gulls almost anywhere. Gulls are symbols of the wild ocean and of storms. They are friends of the farmer, denizens of the city dumps, and the scourge of the airports. In flight they are unforgettably graceful.

Long wings and streamlined bodies contribute to the gull's remarkable flight capability. The feet are held straight back to reduce drag from the air.

The World of the Gull

If you travel the world over, you can see gulls in the bleak frozen wastes of the Arctic, on the burning sand beaches of Arabia, among the storm clouds of Tierra del Fuego, on all the shores of America. They live around the lakes in Ohio, Louisiana, and Utah and in the fields of the Great Plains following the farmers and their plows. Wherever you see them, they will be "doing their thing"—using every opportunity offered by land and water for gaining their livelihood and pursuing their varied ways of life.

Gulls are true opportunists. Equipped by extraordinary flying ability, cooperativeness, intelligence, and enviable digestive capacities, they live strange and wonderful lives. These masters of the wind and the elements are at home on the prairies, where grasshoppers and other insects abound. They give the eastern shore at Gloucester its character, along with the tingling aroma of salt air, tar, and codfish brought in from the sea in boats. Their haunting cries rise above the thunder of the booming surf of the Pacific coast. They soar gracefully over the sandy beach at Galveston, where ships come in from the Gulf of Mexico bringing bananas, fish, jute bagging, and oil from distant lands which the gulls have already seen in their travels. Their discordant screaming alerts the passengers of the ferry out of Anacortes, Washington, as they pass the rocky islands where thousands of gulls are raising their young.

Gulls each day fly with ships between Victoria, British Columbia, and Port Angeles, Washington.

Meet the Gull

Wherever gulls live, they not only accept opportunity when it first appears, but they look for opportunity. They are cooperative. They find food by watching one another.

Their many abilities contribute to their success in life. They can walk, fly, and swim with ease, which is not true of most birds. These capabilities put them in touch with food items that vary from cherries, mice, brine fly larvae, wheat, and steak bones, to eggs, young ducks, and earthworms.

The majority of gull species inhabit the ocean shores or the borders of lakes and large rivers. As "edge" birds, they live where land and water meet. Thus they have the opportunity of finding food in two environments. Even those that live inland are capable of long flights if better feeding grounds are needed.

In migration, most gulls follow the coasts, where they can fish in the sea or live on the bounty of human wastefulness on land. They can eat a lot when opportunity comes. An expandable bill, a large gullet, and a holding capacity that equals one-third or more of the bird's weight enable the gull to satisfy its ravenous appetite.

Gulls, our most valuable scavenger birds, help keep our beaches and harbors clean. They are among the most widely distributed birds in the world. Of the forty-four recognized species, twenty-nine breed in the Northern Hemisphere. One species or another lives at least a part of the year in every state in the Union.

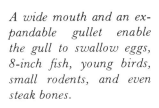

A wide mouth and an expandable gullet enable the gull to swallow eggs, 8-inch fish, young birds, small rodents, and even steak bones.

The drama and beauty of bird flight illustrated by the gull.

Gulls are long-winged, web-footed water birds that belong to the order Charadriiformes (shorebirds, gulls, auks, and allies) and the family Laridae (gulls and terns). The more common species are recognized as gulls by most people. There is great variation in the plumage of different gulls, which is exhibited in shades of grays and white. Some species have black heads. Others have brown markings. At least one species, the glaucous gull of the Arctic, is pure white. The gull best known to people of the eastern United States is the herring gull, a bird nearly twice as large as a crow and marked with gray on the back, black wing tips, a white head, and a yellow bill.

Gulls are adapted to the climates and food supplies of many lands. Ten feet from my office window in downtown Portland, Oregon, one large western gull appeared daily at noon over a period of three winters, in anticipation of the lunch scraps people tossed to his stone ledge. In London, a few years ago, I saw black-headed gulls flying beneath the Tower Bridge to catch pieces of bread and cheese tossed into the air by tourists standing on the bank of the Thames.

One unusual gull, the Andean gull, breeds on the shores of Lake Titicaca more than twelve thousand feet high in the Andes of South

America. The Patagonian black-headed gull in Tierra del Fuego raises its young in the stormy land of the southern seas. The ivory gull breeds north of the Arctic Circle and winters over the drift ice and pack ice of Greenland, Labrador, and the northern coast of Siberia.

The black-legged kittiwake (another unusual gull) is preeminently a bird of the sea. It is common in the North Atlantic (and off the North Pacific coast), where it follows ships day after day, and also wanders to the coasts of Europe, Africa, and Japan. Gulls thus are adapted to live in summer heat or Arctic cold, to cross oceans, and to associate with men when it is to their advantage.

In the vicinity of New York, as many as 200,000 herring gulls, known to many people in the eastern United States as the "sea gull," do scavenger feeding in garbage dumps and along the wharves. Gulls go inland without hesitation when food becomes abundant in populated districts. At times they are quite fearless. In Portland, Oregon, they gather in parks and on school grounds where earthworms are abundant in the lawns. They pay little heed to people who walk among them, or to school children at play.

Gulls not only show little fear of men but are aggressive among them-

Gulls soaring on the wind with hardly noticeable wing movements.

selves. Although they are social birds, especially when nesting in large colonies, they bicker with one another and show animosity toward their neighbors, including herons, pelicans, cormorants, and other birds that nest near their colonies. When their chicks are young and helpless, the adults guard them constantly to keep neighbor gulls from killing them.

Much of the gull's behavior is influenced by stimuli from the outer world. As Niko Tinbergen points out in *The Herring Gull's World*, the innate behavior of gulls shows great adaptability but astonishing limitations. Gulls, for example, instinctively drop clams and crabs on rocks, highways, and bridges to break the shells, but they also repeatedly drop shellfish on soft mud or sand and do not appear to distinguish between hard and soft surfaces.

Gulls have memories for certain places and things. After months of wandering, mates recognize each other when they return to the breeding grounds. They also know each other's voice, and a few days after their chicks are hatched they know their own young among all the thousands of other young in the colony.

Some species of gulls also have exceptional homing ability. G. V. T. Matthews, in his investigations of orientation ability, found that the lesser black-backed gull, which is common in England, readily returned to its home territory even when taken to regions which normally it never visits. Other migratory gulls memorize landmarks and as they grow older learn to take shorter routes when returning from their wintering grounds to their breeding areas.

The social nature of gulls is best exhibited when they nest in great colonies on large rocks in the sea, on sandy islands in desert lakes, or in marshlands in the prairies. The habits of some species during the breeding and nesting season, particularly those of the herring gull, have provided fine opportunities for scientists to study their courtship displays, the instinctive reactions of gull chicks to bill color of the adults, and the attributes by which gulls recognize members of their own species.

In general, gulls are monogamous and keep the same mates year after

Gulls fly in formation to conserve energy. They also fly in groups when food has been sighted.

year. These mates come together each spring at the beginning of the nesting season and become a part of the social life of the colony. On the nesting grounds, gull society has many facets and is characterized by much status seeking.

The older gulls have the highest standing socially and there is a gradation of rank from the oldest to the youngest. Even gulls that are one or two years old must keep their necks pulled in. A lifted head is an invitation to battle, and the older gull, because of its size and experience, usually wins. Status in gull society is ever changing, since a few members are always working their way up in social standing.

Courtship, territorial establishment, and even fights are highly ceremonial in the world of the gull. The voices of gulls have different meanings. Gulls know the invisible boundaries that surround the 5 to 10 square feet of ground on which a couple lives. And, unlike human youngsters, gull chicks must stay in their own yards or suffer the penalty of a whack on

19

the head or of being struck dead by the parents of neighboring young.

In spite of the stern rules of behavior in gull society, the birds are much attached to their breeding grounds. Their society is exclusive of most other water birds with similar colonial habits. They do not nest within the colonies of murres, guillemots, cormorants, or pelicans. The very density of populations in gull colonies precludes invasion of their territory by all but the most audacious of bird predators, such as the skuas, crows, and falcons.

The attributes of gulls for successful living are fascinating in their number and diversity. The gull itself is admirably equipped by flight ability, cooperativeness, and physical structure to cope with the multifarious diets offered by nature and man. Methods of finding food vary with conditions that prevail during any given time of the day and in different seasons.

Through the years, I have observed that the western gulls and the glaucous-winged gulls along the Oregon coast are well aware of the tides and their effect on food gathering. At low tide, when much of the beach is exposed, they spend a great deal of time walking at the edge of the water. Then many worms, crustaceans, and clams are accessible. When the tide is high, they sit on rocky prominences or on pilings near the wharves waiting for the salmon fishermen to return and clean their catches.

When storms wash ashore starfishes, mollusks, and seaweeds with their attached animal life, the gulls are busy scavenging regardless of the weather. They eat dead seals, if the hide is broken so that they can get at the contents. Dead sea birds, such as the murres, ducks, and cormorants, are eaten only as a last choice, possibly because of the difficulty in tearing them apart.

The gulls also make a successful living because of their aptitude for wandering over a wide local territory. When the storms are severe along the Oregon coast, the wintering gulls move inland to the grassy pastures where dairy cattle graze. Near Tillamook, Oregon, I have counted more than a thousand gulls in one 40-acre pasture pulling up water-soaked leaves and grass debris in order to find worms and insects. If snow comes in with a Pacific storm and covers the ground, the gulls then migrate to the garbage dumps near Portland.

In addition to their adaptability to weather changes, gulls have other attributes that enable them to live well. Their omnivorousness, for example, is exhibited from the Arctic regions to the tropics. Clarence Cottam, in an article "Gulls as Vegetarians," lists various gull foods of vegetable origin. California gulls eat sprouting barley. Franklin gulls feed extensively on wheat and other grains when insects are scarce. Herring gulls cause damage to blueberry crops in Maine and glaucous gulls eat marine algae in Alaska.

Because gulls can drink either fresh or salt water, they are able to live on land or sea. Most animals cannot excrete salt, but gulls have a pair of glands above the eyes that handle the problem nicely. These glands, which become enlarged when gulls drink seawater, flush the salt from their systems through openings in the bill. This mechanism probably contributes to the success with which California gulls live in salt marshes in the vicinity of Great Salt Lake, Utah.

Looking for worms and insects in wet grassland near Tillamook, Oregon. Gulls lift clumps of grass and debris to find small hidden animals.

The World of the Gull

Structurally, the gull is built to engulf an astonishing amount of food when the opportunity occurs. Durward L. Allen, in "Seaside Freeloader," calls the gull an "airborne meat-bag" and hints that its digestive juices have a capability similar to that of aqua regia. Although his statement is a bit overdrawn, I can agree that a gull has a most remarkable food-handling ability.

Recently, at Siletz Bay on the Oregon coast, I saw a western gull catch nine smelt in less than fifteen minutes at the edge of the fisherman's wharf. These little fish, also being caught by small boys, averaged about 5 inches in length. The gull flew with its full meal to a nearby piling and stood there for three-quarters of an hour. Then suddenly, when the boys started to throw away the entrails of several rock bass they were cleaning, the gull was back on the water eating the leavings in competition with numerous companions.

Much of the gull's instinctive behavior, from hatching to old age, has survival value. From the earliest hours of the gull's life, when as a chick it pecks at its parents' bills—a form of begging that elicits regurgitation of

Gulls dip for food thrown on the water. They seldom dive like ducks, murres, or cormorants and rarely dive from the air.

Gulls are vociferous and voice their displeasure if a favorite observation point is taken by another gull.

partially digested food from the adults—communication between gulls is an important survival factor. The voice, in particular, is much used in communication and has many meanings.

Those of us who live by the sea associate the cries of the gulls with the storms and the booming of the surf. Gull voices there seem to be a challenge to all nature. Other people who live inland, near desert lakes and on the prairies, know the quacking of the smaller gulls. The rare person who sees gulls at their nesting sites and hears the low throaty notes of mating birds knows that the voice of the gull has many subtle variations.

The larger gulls, such as the herring gull, the glaucous-winged gull, and the California gull, are vociferous. Being aggressive birds, they emit hoarse, strident screeches in combat or when competing for food. And yet, the notes of some of these gulls are at times almost musical.

Gull voices are described in the literature in many ways. Their notes are written as *kah, kah, kah,* or *ka-ka-kak.* The call of Heermann's gull, which passes the summer and fall on the coast in the Pacific Northwest, is a high-pitched *whee-ee.* Ralph Hoffman, in *Birds of the Pacific States,* writes that they also utter a whining or cackling note when in flocks. In contrast, the note of the little Bonaparte gull is described as a rough *cherr.*

Personally, I have never been able to construct an auditory image of gull voices from the written descriptions. But if one deliberately associates gull calls with the activities of the birds, their cries and their more plaintive notes become meaningful and are easily retained in memory.

Niko Tinbergen describes one of the common calls of the herring gull as a loud *kleew,* which is answered by other gulls. The meaning of this "call note" is not clear, but it may serve the purpose of informing gulls of the whereabouts of other gulls.

The trumpeting call, consisting of several notes, serves as a challenge to other gulls. The mew call has a mournful sound and is given during the nesting season. It is a note with special meaning between mates and also is given when the gull is hungry. A sound described as *huoh-huoh-huoh-huoh* by Tinbergen is the choking call. It is used both in nest building and during conflicts with other gulls. Sometimes it precedes regurgitation of food for a mate.

In a published study of the breeding ecology of the glaucous-winged gull, Kees Vermeer notes that the mew call, alarm call, and other sounds of this gull on the breeding ground on Mandarte Island, British Columbia, do not differ qualitatively from those described by Tinbergen for the herring gull. During my boat trips past this island the cacophony that reaches my ears leaves me with the impression that the whole island is an area of discord; this, however, is only one part of the whole business of gulls' raising their young.

On the breeding grounds the cries of gulls never cease. I have listened to the piercing calls of multitudes of gulls on the off-shore islands of the Pacific coast and on Anaho Island in Pyramid Lake, Nevada. The mating calls, alarm calls, attack calls, and begging calls leave no doubt that the

A model of streamlining. Note the large wingspread, the feet folded under the tail, and the legs buried in feathers.

gulls live in a raucous society in which behavior is conditioned both by instinctive individual activity and by the activities of multitudes of fellow gulls. In his report on *The Bird Life of Great Salt Lake*, William H. Behle writes that the California gulls on their breeding ground on Gunnison Island are active and continue to call through the night.

There is always much coming and going from the breeding grounds. Gulls return to their islands to spend the night after long forays over land or sea in search of food. Their proficiency in flight is so great that distance has minor effect on their daily and seasonal movements. The gulls in the Pacific Northwest fly regularly one hundred miles or more, about the countryside and between Portland, Oregon, and the sea coast. Many follow the Columbia River to the sea but others fly directly over the Coast Range. The seasonal migrations of gulls, of course, also attest to their remarkable flight capabilities.

Gulls in flight display many of the characteristics that aid in their identification. When the wings are outstretched, windows or white spots in the darker coloring of the wing tips are diagnostic features that aid in the naming of certain gulls. Size, color markings, and the patterns of color on backs and heads often are distinctive, as are the colors of the legs, which may be green, yellow, or flesh colored.

Gull identification, however, can be enormously difficult because of the differences between juvenile plumages and adult plumages and because of seasonal changes in the feather colors of adults. The wing tips of some gulls show characteristic markings. The herring gull, for example, has black wing tips with "mirrors," which are rounded white spots back of the tips of the primary feathers.

Size of the bird may be a diagnostic characteristic: the ring-billed gull resembles the herring gull, but is smaller and has a black ring around the bill. The shape of the tail is also apparent in flight. Most gulls have rounded tails which are somewhat fan-shaped. Ross's gull, however, has a wedge-shaped tail; and Sabine's gull has a forked tail.

Wing patterns, color of bodies, black heads of certain species such as Bonaparte's gull, and even the color of the eye ring are other useful characteristics for gull identification. Some of the better bird guides have keys or charts which compare the attributes of different species of gulls commonly found together. But in spite of all the published aids, gull identification can be difficult because of changing juvenile gull plumages, which may continue for three or four years before the bird becomes mature, and because of seasonal changes in the plumage of the adults.

Some of the larger gulls are almost identical except for eye color and color of the eye ring. Neal Griffith Smith, in "Visual Isolation in Gulls," describes the visual signals and eye characteristics by which four kinds of Arctic gulls differentiate themselves. The large glaucous gull's eye has a yellow iris and a bright yellow eye-ring. The herring gull has a yellow iris but an orange eye-ring. Thayer's gull, which is listed by some authorities as a subspecies of the herring gull, has a dark brown iris and a reddish-purple eye-ring. Kumlien's gull, the smallest of the associated group of Arctic gulls, and considered a variety of the Iceland gull, has an iris that varies from clear yellow to dark brown. Its eye-ring is reddish-purple.

The body structure and habits of some gulls are comparatively unique. The swallow-tailed gull of the Galapagos Islands, for example, has a notched tail and is the only nocturnal gull. Its pointed wings and manner of flight give the appearance of a swallow or tern.

Most gulls do not have singular characteristics such as notched tails; instead, they must be distinguished from one another by sex, age, size, bill,

Most of our common gulls have square tails, though some are rounded. The tail of Sabine's gull is forked; that of Ross's gull is wedge-shaped.

feet, and color patterns. Jonathan Dwight, in *The Gulls (Laridae) of the World; Their Plumages, Moults, Variations, Relationships and Distribution*, summed up these differences many years ago.

The sexes are alike in most gulls, although the males of some species are larger than the females and have heavier bills. Increasing age produces many changes in shape of the primaries, or main flight feathers along the outer edge of the wings, pattern of the tail, color of the bill and legs, and color and pattern of body plumage. One of the fascinating phases of gull watching is to learn and recognize these changes in the gulls that inhabit one's home locality.

Gulls differ greatly in size. Each wing of the great black-backed gull, for example, may be 20 inches in length. The bird itself may be 2 ½ feet from tip of bill to tip of tail. Other large gulls are the California gull, herring gull, and the glaucous-winged gull. Heermann's gull, the Japanese gull which ranges the coast of Asia, and the ring-billed gull which winters on both coasts of North America are examples of medium-sized gulls.

Gulls form pairs before the mating season. Some of these pairs remain together during the winter.

Sabine's gull, the common kittiwake, and the silver gull which ranges from the coasts of South Africa to New Zealand and Australia are small gulls. The little gull, commonly seen in Europe, is the smallest of them all. Its total length is less than 12 inches and each wing is less than 9 inches.

Bill variation in gulls is marked, ranging in size from large and stout to small and slender. Color varies from yellow to red or reddish to black. Some gulls have bills banded with black or yellow or red. Some have bills with red spots near the tip. The bills of gull chicks are usually flesh colored and become black during the first year.

Leg and foot color is an important characteristic in gull identification. Legs vary from flesh colored to yellow, red, black, gray, or greenish. In observing gulls for this trait, even with a binocular, I find that the apparent color changes with the quality and intensity of light. Sunlight is best; in stormy weather, when gulls are active, I never feel certain about my judgment of the color of gull feet. Leg color is best observed when gulls are standing or walking, since their legs are usually hidden in feathers during flight.

Gulls search for food left by people who picnic along the seashore. If one finds food they all scramble to be in on the feast.

The mantle, which includes the back and some of the wing feathers, is usually gray and is one of the most characteristic features of the common gulls. The color varies from pearly gray to lead gray, or deep slate gray. A few gulls, such as the glaucous gull and its smaller relative the Iceland gull, have white backs. The Aden gull, which wanders along the coasts of Arabia, Africa, and India, is the only gull with a brown mantle.

One would have to be a great traveler to follow their migrations and to go around the year with the gulls. The Franklin gulls, for example, nest on the northern prairies and spend their winters on the coast of Chile. The California gulls breed on islands in northern Canada, in Great Salt

Lake, and on islands in other desert lakes of the Southwest. In winter they move to the Pacific coast and to the Gulf Coast of Texas.

Gulls of the Southern Hemisphere, such as the Magellan gull, move north from their nesting grounds near the tip of South America to winter along the coasts of Chile and Argentina. Their winter is our summer. The black-legged kittiwake, outside of its breeding territory in the Arctic regions, is a wanderer of the sea, where it ranges from Japan to Europe, Africa, and North America. Even in this jet age, one would be hard put to follow it all around the year.

People who travel extensively can meet gulls in almost any part of the world, for the lives of these birds involve nesting, raising their young, flocking together in search of food, then migrations in fall and spring to localities suited to their needs, as well as local explorations during all seasons of the year.

During my sixteen years in the Pacific Northwest, I watched more than a dozen species of gulls come and go with the seasons. Some of these nested in Oregon, Washington, and British Columbia. Others passed through on their semiannual migrations, while still others spent either the winter or the summer and then were gone for the rest of the year. The activities of these gulls—most of which are common and widely known, at least among confirmed bird watchers—have given me the general picture of gull life throughout the year without my having to travel around the world.

Many of my memorable experiences with gulls at the edge of the sea are the result of the lure of the Three Arch Rocks near Oceanside, Oregon. The Arch Rocks have been set aside as one of our National Wildlife Refuges. Scarcely a mile from land, they are three forbidding cliffs in the midst of the turbulent sea, where a great bird drama begins in the spring of each year.

There the gulls live where the murres are assembled like a white-shirt-fronted choir. Living near them are petrels, guillemots, kittiwakes, and tufted puffins. Cormorants sit in rows on Storm Rock when the sea is not breaking too high. On my boat tours across the heaving waters around

Meet the Gull

Shag Rock and Middle Arch Rock, the chorus of a million bird voices, mingled with the roars of tawny-coated sea lions, always gives me a priceless experience in a world that still is wild. Happily, these birds, and the gulls, are protected from the heavy impact of man's tinkering with nature.

The flight of the gull is one of the most pleasing sights in nature. Three Arch Rocks in the background are used by gulls for nesting and roosting. This is a Pacific coast wildlife refuge and the birds there are safe from human interference.

Spring

SPRING IN THE gulls' world has many faces. In the Arctic regions, where some of the gulls remain throughout the year, the ice breaks up along the continental margins only when summer has come for most of us. By April's end the glaucous gulls follow open spaces in the sea and cross large areas of ice to reach the rocky cliffs where they and the kittiwakes nest together.

Along our own shores numerous species of gulls find an abundant supply of winter food in the marine zone and the nearby coastal towns and cities. They move in various directions to their breeding areas with the coming of spring.

In equatorial waters, the swallow-tailed gull, for example, spends the entire year roaming among the Galapagos Islands and makes no definite migration in spring. The silver gulls in Australia move south along the coasts to their breeding grounds in the season that is our autumn. Along the South American coasts many of the gulls make southward flights in October and November.

Most of the gulls we know move in leisurely flight northward along the coasts with the advance of spring. The California gulls leave their winter quarters on the Pacific coast and migrate inland to lakes in the western desert, where islands give them protection for the nesting season that continues into summer. The gulls that truly come north with the spring are the little Franklin's gulls that make the long journey from the coast of

Opposite: Salt Lake City monument to the California gulls that devoured crickets and saved Mormon crops in 1848.

Immature gull. Three years are required before adult plumage is developed by the larger species.

Chile to their breeding grounds in the marshes in the central prairie in southern Canada.

Spring heralds the inland arrival of many gulls. When I lived in the Great Lakes country, the flocks of herring gulls grew larger in March and their raucous calls foretold the time when they would begin their community life of courtship, egg laying, and raising of young. During a year I spent in Utah, the return of the adult California gulls began in late February and continued well into May. Even when snow still covered the ground, their harsh voices and pre-nesting-season flights over the marshes northwest of Ogden were among the most evident harbingers of spring.

In the Pacific Northwest the glaucous-winged gulls, western gulls, and ring-billed gulls, so numerous in winter in the parks and garbage dumps of the large cities, depart for their breeding grounds in the San Juan Islands, Alaska, and northern Canada. In late spring, however, when these gulls

34

are gone, Heermann's gulls begin to arrive from their nesting territories in Mexico and Baja California. A few come in late May and they become numerous in midsummer.

Along the Atlantic coast the herring gulls start northward in early spring. Some of them nest in northern New York or Maine, and south along the Atlantic coast to New Jersey, Maryland, and Virginia. Others fly as far as Labrador, where the cod and its bait, the capelin, and millions of clams and other sea creatures provide delectable food for the adult gulls and their young.

The herring gulls that fly to Labrador do not hurry on their northward journey. Ice sometimes fills the harbors until late May. Although they leave their winter territories early in March, they migrate slowly with many side trips inland for food. Those around the Great Lakes also make inland excursions in search of food. Some remain until the spring plowing exposes worms and insects in the farmers' fields. At night they return and rest in great flocks on the dunes or on lakes. If they take sanctuary

Gulls are expert swimmers but dive less expertly than murres, auks, or cormorants.

in the water, their dense plumage protects them from the cold and keeps them afloat. But the flocks gradually diminish in size as they depart for the north to begin their nesting season toward the end of May.

Gulls nest in many places in the United States. California gulls use breeding grounds in the marshes of eastern Oregon and northern Utah. Along with white pelicans, they nest on Anaho Island in Pyramid Lake northeast of Reno, Nevada. Surprisingly, they also are known to breed in company with ring-billed gulls and herring gulls on Pelican Island in Dog Lake, Manitoba.

The Heermann's gulls, seen so frequently along the Oregon coast from June to August, are post-breeding wanderers from their nesting grounds in Mexico and Baja California. Some of these, along with the brown pelicans, nest along the coast of Central America and then move northward as far as British Columbia in autumn.

The small and pretty black-headed Franklin's gulls, after spending their winter along the shores of the Gulf of Mexico from Louisiana to Panama, and along the coast of South America from northern Peru to southern Chile and Patagonia, return north to their nesting grounds in Alberta and Manitoba, Canada, and in Utah, the Dakotas, Iowa, and Oregon. On the Malheur Wildlife Refuge in eastern Oregon, I always enjoy seeing them searching for insect food in the flooded meadows among flocks of Canada geese, curlews, and yellow-headed blackbirds.

Another black-headed gull—Sabine's gull—along with the all-white ivory gull, arrives at its breeding grounds in the Spitzbergen-Franz Joseph region and in other Arctic areas in June. Their colonies are located on steep cliffs and small islands. The Eskimos, according to Peter Freuchen and Finn Salomonsen, report that they nest in great numbers in the interior of northwestern Baffin Island.

Wherever gulls nest, their colonies usually are characterized by great numbers of birds. William H. Behle states that California gulls in northern Utah are so numerous that exaggerated estimates of hundreds of thousands have been made regarding their presence on Hat Island. Other estimates have placed the numbers at fifteen to twenty thousand. Behle, however, estimated a population of about eighty thousand adults concentrated in a few colonies.

On Little Galloo Island in eastern Lake Ontario, Ralph S. Palmer, in May, 1955, estimated forty-five thousand ring-billed gull nests on a 20-acre area, a density of approximately two thousand nests per acre. Other investigators report populations of two gull nests per square yard. These numbers, of course, do not compare with those of the murres and other sea birds that nest so close together on rocky cliffs that they almost touch one another.

In spite of the multitudes of gulls in breeding colonies, there is organization instead of chaos in their spring and summer worlds. Before they arrive on their nesting grounds, whether they are the sand dunes of Holland, a dry desert island in a Nevada lake, or the off-shore rocks of the Oregon or Newfoundland coasts, some of the gulls meet former mates.

Murres nest so close together that gulls steal their eggs with difficulty. (Oregon Game Commission photo)

Nesting grounds of ring-billed and California gulls, Klamath Lake, Oregon. (Oregon Game Commission photo)

On the breeding grounds, colony organization evolves gradually, since all the gulls do not arrive at once. In March and April, the gulls in the Pacific Northwest, for example, gradually leave their inland feeding areas around Portland, Tillamook, and other coastal cities. Some migrate to far northern colonies. But the western gulls that breed along the coast sail in endless processions up and down the edge of the surf, or pass in long files over the dunes near Florence, Oregon, or around the windswept rocky points that offer them airlift where the sea winds rise from the water over wooded

Gulls wade in the surf at low tide when small animals are uncovered by the waves.

hills. Their harsh screaming and quarreling portend the coming of the nuptial season and more vociferous days ahead when they will establish their social groups and raise their young.

Gulls that nest along the Pacific coast prefer the safety of islands, where men and mammal predators are not likely to be present. The rocks or "sea stacks" in the Pacific Ocean near Bandon, Oregon, for example, are homes for gulls, murres, and puffins. These last two birds, of course, get their food from the sea. But the gulls that nest on Sphinx, Great Stone Face,

39

and other rocks, frequent the wharves and explore the beach for crabs, dead animals, and fishes. They appear when clam diggers start their work. They also frequent the Coquille and other coastal rivers when small fish are numerous.

In May the western gulls along the Oregon coast assemble on sites near or adjacent to colonies of nesting cormorants and murres. Here again is a source of food, since the gulls raid the neighboring bird colonies for eggs and young which they snatch from unguarded nests. Sometimes the gulls harass the murres in pairs until one gull gets the egg and shares it with his fellow pirate. The sea-bird population is not decimated by these gull depredations, since the victims simply lay more eggs and resume nesting.

Adult gulls tend to return to the same colonies and the same nesting sites for successive breeding seasons. Some pairs stay mated for years. It is generally believed that mates recognize one another even on the flight from winter quarters to their spring and summer living areas. Often in early spring, on the migration flight, gull mates pursue one another through the sky. Sometimes the male presents the female with a fish and she bows and responds in tones that must sound musical to her mate.

Courtship in the gull world has many facets and varies among species. California gulls indulge in a dance routine that includes pecking, sparring, neck stretching, and bill rubbing. Like other gulls, the male sometimes regurgitates food and the female accepts part of the offering, not infrequently consenting to mate at that time.

Herring gulls are sometimes quite ceremonious in their courtship, which lasts even through the nest-building period. Together the mates collect dried weed stems and grass, which they drop on the ground. Occasionally the female sits on the nest and arranges the dried material in a circle around her body. But her attention is not wholly on nest building. She nibbles at her mate's neck and bill and sometimes participates with him in a dance, in which the two gulls face one another with necks outstretched and bodies tilted forward. While they are dancing they also sing a strange, low-pitched, gurgling song. This ritual of life includes feeding of the female by the male.

Gulls in general are monogamous and remain paired for life. If one dies, it is believed that the remaining gull takes a new mate in the next season. The initial courtship, when young gulls pair for the first time, is begun by the female. Tinbergen states that the herring gull female "proposes" by walking toward a male, her head and body in horizontal position, voicing a melodious call as she tosses her head and walks in a circle around him.

The male responds by making himself large and by looking around for other, threatening, males. Or he indulges in neck gyrations and re-gurgitates food, which the female immediately eats. Fighting, nest build-ing, and feeding are common activities associated with courtship and pair formation.

Love affairs between gulls are sometimes amusing to the observer. Occa-sionally the male appears to practice a form of studied indifference to the attentions of the aggressive female. He ignores her presence and even her attempts to push him with her body or to rub her neck against his. A vigor-

Franklin's gulls form pairs before the nesting season and hunt for food together. The blackbird is searching for insects in the wet meadow.

Nesting ground of western gulls. Alert sentinels are always on guard while other members of the colony fly away to obtain food.

ous peck with her bill changes his attitude and sometimes triggers a wild chase on the ground and in the air. This chase culminates in many caresses and an exchange of cooing or mewing sounds that only a gull can understand.

After pair formation, the male usually establishes the territory where the nest will be built. In colonies where hundreds or even thousands of gulls nest and raise their young, boundary clashes are inevitable. The male is usually more aggressive in fighting off intruders that cross the invisible boundary of his domain. The female also jabs at owners of neighboring territories and issues warnings to stay out by pulling grass or charging the intruder, especially if it lands too close to her mate. Boundary disputes frequently excite many neighbors, and the loud calls of the spectators become contagious until the tumult of trumpeting spreads throughout the colony.

Spring

Different species of gulls, of course, have different habits and select different kinds of breeding grounds. Laughing gulls, the only gulls that breed in the state of Louisiana, nest in depressions in the sand in the midst of trash and debris at the mouths of the Mississippi River. Ring-billed gulls nest on stony or rocky shores in far northern lands. The herring gulls, California gulls, western gulls, and other large gulls that most of us know are the colonial nesters and the ones that have given us the best insight into gull society and the ways in which they raise their young.

The little Franklin's gull, so common in the prairie regions, makes its nest of dead rushes in wet marshes in parts of our northern states and in southern Canada. Around the marshy sloughs and lakes they fly in clouds of thousands. In contrast, the Bonaparte's gull nests in trees in the far northwest and the interior of Alaska.

When gulls are paired and their territories are established, nest building is by both sexes. The herring gull, for example, usually lays three eggs and each parent takes its turn sitting on the nest. By the time eggs are hatched some twenty-six days later, the nest has become larger, since each bird brings in additional material whenever it relieves its mate.

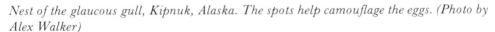

Nest of the glaucous gull, Kipnuk, Alaska. The spots help camouflage the eggs. (Photo by Alex Walker)

Western gull eggs hatching. Only one chick may survive.

The eggs of gulls show great variation. The ground color of herring gull eggs varies from olive drab to light blue to cinnamon, with markings of brown, gray, or lilac. The ground color of California gull eggs varies from light to dark greenish browns to gray or buff, evenly marked with blotches of irregular size and shapes of light brown or gray. These decorations give protective coloration but do not prevent occasional thefts by other gulls and such wily predators as crows and ravens.

Young gulls "pip" the egg by chipping a hole in the shell with an egg tooth at the tip of the bill. Emergence of the chick may require from twenty minutes to more than ten hours. The wet and bedraggled youngster is brooded by the parent until its downy feathers are dry. It moves about

Glaucous-winged gull chick.

beneath its parent and is soon able to stand and walk. Then its adventures in the gull world begin.

One of the first instinctive actions of the chick is to peck at the bills of its parents. In the herring gull the aiming point is the red spot on the parent's mandible. The chicks do not always hit on the first try, but when they succeed, the parent regurgitates food which is held in the bill and presented to the chick. After this first feeding, the chick rapidly learns how to beg for food.

Gull chicks show different types of feeding behavior, depending on the species. Laughing gulls, for example, peck at the bill of the parent and then grasp the bill and stroke it downward. After several pecks, the parent regurgitates partially digested food and drops it on the ground. The chick then pecks the food, tears away pieces, and swallows them.

The feeding behavior of laughing gull chicks, studied in detail by Jack P. Hailman, appears to be an instinct not fully developed at birth. At first the chick is inexperienced, but it learns to peck accurately by practice. Hailman believes that the chick does not recognize food, but by pecking the bills of adults and getting results it strikes food and learns to recognize it. His experiments indicate that much still remains to be learned about innate releasing mechanisms that contribute to the survival of gulls and various other animals.

In the gull city, chicks soon exhibit many other behavioral activities, which serve to protect them from enemies, including gulls of their own kind. If they stray into the adjoining territory of other gulls, they are liable to be struck dead and eaten. When alarmed by the passing of large gulls such as the great black-backed gull, they flatten out on the moss or grass

Gull chicks are spotted when young. These western gull babies blend nicely with their background. (Photo by Alex Walker)

and even bury their heads, since their bills and eyes are more conspicuous than their spotted bodies.

The early days in the life of a gull chick are uncertain and it has many adventures. The parents recognize their own young and vigorously defend them against other gulls and outside intruders, including man. I have never been hit by a gull defending its chicks, but have had a few dive close to my head. William H. Behle has had his hat knocked off several times by gulls. A student of his, while banding young California gulls, received an inch-long laceration on his scalp from the dive of an adult.

Gull chicks apparently learn to recognize the voices of their parents. C. G. Beer found that laughing gull chicks answered the call of their parents and approached them. The calls of other laughing gulls caused the chicks to withdraw and sit or crouch. The chicks develop the ability to recognize their parents during the first days after hatching, when they associate the parental calls with feeding.

As gull chicks grow larger they become more adventuresome and wander about in the parental territory. If they cross the boundary, or are left unguarded, they may be pecked on the head by neighboring gulls and quickly learn that too much wandering is dangerous. If the young gull can survive to the age of six weeks, the age at which many young herring gulls first fly, it stands a good chance of returning to the colony with a mate in future years and starting a family of its own.

Young gulls are adept at avoiding exposure to the elements, especially when the rookery occupies barren peninsulas, rocky slopes, or hot sandy islands. The chicks of California gulls, for example, seek the shade of sagebrush and saltbush plants that grow on the islands in the desert lakes of Nevada. Western gull chicks in Baja California, and on the desert islands in the Gulf of California, take advantage of shelter afforded by rocks, crevices, and pieces of debris. George A. Bartholomew and William R. Dawson report that they avail themselves of small patches of shade that shelter only their heads. In one instance the chicks used a sea lion's carcass for escape from the intense rays of the sun.

The World of the Gull

Since young gulls are not closely attended by their parents, they spend much time wandering about in their own back yards. Their activities contribute to rapid development of physical strength. As they become fully feathered they spend much time stretching and beating their wings. Soon they are able to rise vertically and then can progress horizontally by leaping and flapping at the same time. In July, most young gulls develop proficiency in flight and set forth in youthful gangs to forage for themselves.

Foraging in spring and early summer during the nesting season occupies a large part of the adult gull's time. The parent gulls must feed themselves, and occasionally their mates upon the nest. After the chicks are hatched, an amazing diversity of food is brought to the breeding ground.

On sandy coasts the gulls walk up and down the beach. In the shallow

Western gull chick recently hatched. The mother broods her chicks until their down is dry. Then they are less liable to attack by adult gulls in the colony. (Photo by Alex Walker)

water of the ebb tide they search for clams, crabs, and even barnacles attached to logs that float in from the sea. Near Oceanside, Oregon, I once watched a large western gull make daily trips at low tide to peck and hammer at sea stars exposed below an overhanging cliff. The skeletons of these starfish are tough, but occasionally the gull loosened one from its mooring and succeeded in pecking out the contents.

Gulls are notorious for stealing eggs and eating chicks that belong to other species of birds. Cormorants, murres, guillemots, and terns that nest in the vicinity of gull colonies must be particularly vigilant in protecting their eggs from raids by gulls. Herring gulls and great black-backed gulls are most adept at stealing the eggs and young of smaller gull species.

Gulls, like many other birds whose chicks remain in the nest for a time, remove eggshells soon after the chicks are hatched. This behavioral practice eliminates an attraction for winged predators, since the white inner surface of the shell is more visible than the mottled pattern of the unhatched egg. Niko Tinbergen names some of the penalties for not removing the shells: harmful bacteria may breed in the abandoned shell; the chick may be trapped in the half shell; or it may be injured by the sharp edge of the broken shell.

In his study of black-headed gulls near Ravenglass on the Irish Sea coast of Cumberland, England, Tinbergen observed that pipped eggs and freshly hatched gull chicks were eaten by other gulls in the colony. But dry and fluffy chicks were not eaten by their adult neighbors. The gull parents ordinarily guarded the chicks until they were dry, and delayed up to three hours the removal of shells from the nest.

The food of the gull varies greatly among species and with the availability of food in the nesting locality. California gulls are known to prey heavily on eggs and young of cinnamon teal, redheads, pheasants, and avocets. Cherry growers have complained that gulls knock cherries off the trees. They feed on animals hit on the road by motorists. They follow the plow and consume insect larvae, worms, and small rodents. Clarence Cottam once saw some 2,500 of these gulls feeding on a large species of midge (chironomid) that had emerged from Strawberry Lake in Wasatch County, Utah.

On the northeastern coast of North America, great black-backed gulls make it almost impossible for arctic terns to breed near some gull colonies. Years ago, Johan Beetz described these large gulls as the greatest destroyers of the eider duck, especially when the supply of small fishes was insufficient to feed the gull chicks. The young eider would try to escape by diving, but the gull would follow until the young bird emerged and then seize it with its powerful bill. Sometimes the gull dropped the eider on the rocks and then picked up the dead body.

On the midwestern prairies great flocks of Franklin's gulls follow the plow in search of upturned worms and insects. These same beautiful birds also frequent the edges of northern lakes and streams, where insects are abundant. They appear along the Snake River and the Yellowstone in early summer, hawking the caddis flies like swallows.

In contrast, gulls that live in the polar whiteness—the glaucous gull, Iceland gull, and glaucous-winged gull—have need of larger prey for heat production in the cold of Greenland and the far north. Along with the jaegers and snowy owls, they search the tundra for lemmings in March. In April, when they arrive on the breeding cliffs, they search the seashore for dead fishes, seals, and other animals in the tidal zone. When the kittiwakes arrive to nest in May, they feed on krill and fish fry, which they find by foraging on the open sea.

The breeding grounds of the many species of gulls are scattered throughout the world. The principal locations are listed in the section Gull Genera and Species at the end of this book. The migrations of gulls that bring them back to their nesting colonies is a study in world travel to which birdbanding has contributed a great mass of information.

Birdbanding studies have shown that young gulls become great travelers before they reach breeding age and return to their original homes to reproduce their kind. But even before they leave their nesting sites they begin to undergo many changes in habits, structure, and color. One of the most visible changes is caused by the molt, which results in a plumage cycle that periodically alters the gull's appearance until it becomes adult. Even adults undergo seasonal molts twice each year. Colors of the bill and legs also show seasonal changes: yellow colors and red spots on the bills of some species become intensified for the breeding season.

In his classic work on the gulls of the world, Jonathan Dwight described the various plumage cycles by which species of different sizes change from downy chicks to adults with mature plumage. Mature gulls, by molting twice each year, exhibit a breeding plumage and a winter plumage. These molts and the changing patterns of immature birds make gull identification both fascinating and exasperating.

Large species of gulls, such as the herring gulls, require three years to attain mature plumage. Including the plumage stages following the third year, the molting process is actually a four-year cycle. Medium-sized gulls attain mature plumage within two years (a three-year plumage

Glaucous-winged gull chick. (Oregon Game Commission photo)

cycle). Small species require but one year (a two-year plumage cycle).

The chicks of gulls are covered with down and are similar in pattern and tone. The darker spotting on a grayish or buffy background varies somewhat with the species. The first or juvenal plumage is totally unlike that of adults. Usually it is darker and shows considerable mottling.

Large gulls, after the juvenal stage, go through the following cycle: first winter plumage; first nuptial plumage; second winter plumage; second nuptial plumage; third winter plumage; third nuptial plumage; fourth winter or nonnuptial plumage, at which time they become adults; and fourth nuptial plumage, usually described as the "adult breeding" plumage. In large gulls the brown plumage is assumed a second time, but the bird becomes paler about the head and often grayer on the back. The third winter plumage is essentially that of the adult, but dusky or brownish feathers on the wings and tail may still be visible.

When gulls reach maturity they travel widely in their seasonal territories. They develop remarkable topographic memories and apparently memorize landmarks. On spring and autumn migrations, some species travel thousands of miles and are subject to all the vicissitudes of weather and dangers from enemies on land and sea. If they survive their first year of life, losses are fewer in the second year and more infrequent in subsequent years. The longer a gull lives, the greater its chance for a long life.

Records of gulls living to an age of ten years are numerous. One herring gull in Denmark lived to the age of twenty-eight years. Alfred M. Bailey and Robert J. Niedrach report that a gull banded in Ontario by their friend William Lyon was found dead nineteen years later.* Two captive herring gulls at Morehead City, North Carolina, reported by T. Gilbert Pearson, lived to be forty-five and forty-nine years old, and the female laid eggs once each year for forty-two years. One can hardly imagine the experiences that gulls of this age must have had in their lifetimes.

Editor's Note: Olin Sewall Pettingill, Jr., reported in 1967 that a herring gull banded in Maine lived to an age of thirty-five years, eleven months, and twenty-two days—one of the oldest banded *wild* birds known at the time of the report.

Summer

SUMMER IS BOTH a busy time and a lazy time for gulls. In early summer many gulls, especially those that nest in the far north, are still feeding their young. Later, when the young have learned to fly and have left the breeding grounds, the adults have more time to loiter, preen, explore, or start the wandering that eventually takes them to their autumn and winter quarters.

Gulls find food readily available in summer. Those that fish in large rivers and lakes are not inhibited by ice-covered water. Those that include insects and rodents in their diets find much edible material, since small

Siesta time on sandy beaches of the Pacific Ocean where gulls preen, watch, and rest.

animals are at the height of their reproductive season and therefore are active and abundant. Gulls that follow the sea coasts have a triple abundance of food: fishes from the sea itself; live and dead animals at the tide line, and on the beach; and food provided by the territory inland from the sea, including the edible debris provided by man. The gulls exploit all of these sources of food, since they are great local wanderers with excellent eyesight and the ability to communicate with one another.

The daily travels and activities of gulls in summer seem to be flexible and adapted to food availability, weather, and their own internal physiology. In observing gulls I have often found myself wondering where they go at certain times of the day or night, and how they know almost to the minute when a Gargantuan feed will be available.

The gulls at Depot Bay, on the coast of Oregon, for example, virtually disappear from the vicinity when the boats are out at sea. A few sit on pilings, preening themselves or apparently sleeping. Others cruise up and down the coast or fly out over the Pacific Ocean. Still others visit the large lakes inshore from the sea.

But when the fishermen return to the bay and begin to clean their catch, the gulls seem to appear miraculously to fight and scream over the fish

Gulls perch on poles and high objects where they can watch for food.

offal that is cast into the water. Do sentinel gulls pass the word along that fish are being cleaned? Or do they know which boats carry successful fishermen? I do not know.

Summer at the edge of the sea is a time for great congregations of birds, particularly gulls, pelicans, shearwaters, and murres. Along the Oregon shore, which I explored for many years, a confusion of ocean currents brings the cold deep waters to the surface. The small sea life in these waters attracts great schools of small fishes, which in turn attract larger fishes and the multitudes of birds.

Many of the gulls have not completed their nesting season in midsummer. Consequently such species as the western gulls find good fishing in the cold water near the shore and make constant trips to the sea and back to the gullery with food for their young. The salmon and steelhead fishermen know that gulls are adept at locating schools of smaller fishes and that where the smaller ones are, there the larger fishes will be, feeding upon the small fry.

Not all the gulls that fish the "summer seas" along the northwest coast are local nesting birds. Heermann's gulls migrate north in summer when the nesting season is finished; young and adults both become common

Fishing boats that come in from the sea attract gulls. The birds know that when fish are cleaned they will have food.

around the San Juan Islands in northern Puget Sound. In late June and early July, California and ring-billed gulls leave the inland areas along the Columbia River and become a common sight along the coast. In Puget Sound, mew gulls arrive by mid-August from Alaska and northern Canada. By late summer, Arctic terns and pomarine and parasitic jaegers arrive along the Washington coast. All the migrants are indicative of the widespread post-breeding wandering by gulls and other sea birds as summer begins to merge into autumn.

The edge of the sea, where water meets land, is a prolific source of food for gulls in summer. Low tides are common during the day and sandy beaches are widely exposed, as are the mussel- and barnacle-covered rocks around jutting headlands. The gulls find a large variety of clams, crabs, worms, and other sea creatures. They also eat the scraps of food discarded by tourists, picnic parties, and clam diggers who turn up sand-dwelling creatures with their shovels.

The sea is all-important in the lives of gulls that live in far northern lands. But gull summer in the Arctic is vastly different from summer in the warmer latitudes that most of us know. The season is short and cool. Some of the tidal zones are completely lifeless. And much of the land is waterlogged and covered with lakes.

In the Arctic the ivory gull, glaucous gull, Iceland gull, and glaucous-winged gull are pale or almost white. They exhibit this polar whiteness in common with the polar bear, arctic hare, arctic fox, and the snowy owl.

They also have bird associates and enemies different from those of southern gulls. The sea-bird colonies along the Arctic coasts swarm with thousands of razorbills, murres, black guillemots, terns, jaegers, falcons, fulmars, auks, also king eiders, old squaws, and other ducks. Along with these are other gulls that frequent the ice floes, tidal zones, and breeding cliffs: kittiwakes; Ross's gull, with the rosy tinge on its feathers; the great black-backed gull, marauder in gull and tern colonies; and the little black-headed, fork-tailed, Sabine's gull.

Summer

Foraging by the gulls in the Arctic differs among the species. The glaucous gulls feed on dead fish and other animals of the tidal zone. Kitti-wakes eat small organisms, and capelin and other fishes, which they obtain on flights over the open sea. The parasitic jaegers often rob them of their catch by forcing them to disgorge. The ivory gulls feed mainly as scavengers and pick up pieces of meat left after polar bears have killed a seal. They also eat dead fishes and the blubber and flesh they find around whaling and sealing stations. Other gulls, particularly the herring gulls,

Gulls eat barnacles attached to logs that float in from the sea.

great black-backed gulls, and the glaucous gulls that frequent the sea-bird colonies, slaughter the newly hatched, the fledglings, and the immature birds just learning to fly.

Summer is short for some of the Arctic gulls. A great exodus begins as early as late July and continues on into autumn. Not all gulls fly south. Ross's gulls, after leaving their breeding grounds in eastern Siberia, move northward over the Polar Sea. Where and how they live between October and June is somewhat of a mystery, although they have been seen on the Pribilof Islands in the Bering Sea in winter.

We should also remember that numerous gulls live in the Southern Hemisphere and that their summer is our winter. Many of these gulls go south for their summer breeding season and migrate northward along the coasts of the southern continents in winter. A few do not make extensive migrations. The swallow-tailed gull, for example, is confined to the Galapagos Islands, where it breeds and lays eggs throughout the year. One might say that it lives in perpetual summer.

The gulls of the Southern Hemisphere live mainly along the coasts, although some, such as the Patagonian black-headed gull, breed inland in South America. Other gulls that nest on the South American coasts are the Magellan, Simeon, and southern black-backed gulls. Unlike our Arctic regions, the Antarctic continent has no breeding gulls. The Australian coast has its resident gulls, some of which breed in the subantarctic islands. And the African coast has its gull visitors, some of which nest on the mainland and on islands in the Indian Ocean.

Although most of us will never see the gulls of the southern oceans, and many of us will not see the gulls of our own coasts, there are gulls to be seen in abundance in our inland states. Among these, the little Franklin's gulls are the most delightful beauties of the prairies. Scarcely larger than a domestic pigeon, they move southward in summer from their nesting grounds in Canada to spend the remainder of the warm months catching grasshoppers in the fields and sweeping the skies over prairie cities to capture flying insects. When they are near at hand, the exquisite rosy blush can be seen on their breasts. A dark hood covers the head and neck and the wings are black-tipped. The rest of the plumage is white, with the exception of the gray mantle. These are truly handsome gulls.

People who live near great marshy flats in the far northern prairie see these gulls in multitudes during their nesting season in late spring and early summer. If disturbed or flushed from their platform-like nests of reeds and grass stems built up above the water, the gulls rise from the colony in screaming hordes. But if the intruder remains still for a time, they return and stand above their two or three eggs. When the young are full-fledged, the summer migration begins and the birds wander southward in large flocks.

During the years when I did grassland research in Colorado, Wyoming, and the Dakotas, I saw many ring-billed gulls resting around the shores of prairie and mountain lakes. These gulls, with the black bands around the tips of their bills, were common at all seasons but mostly were non-breeding migrants. I did not see their nesting colonies until I lived in Oregon and visited the Malheur National Wildlife Refuge. There, in the marshlands, the ring-billed gulls nest in company with a vast assemblage of birds, including California gulls, Franklin's gulls, ducks, killdeers, American avocets, black terns, long-billed curlews, Canada geese, and yellow-headed blackbirds.

The California gulls are essentially inland birds in summer, since they nest near fresh water or saline lakes from Great Slave Lake in Canada south to North Dakota and west to Utah, Nevada, and Mono Lake, California. They also nest on Klamath Lake, Oregon, along with great blue herons, ducks, and many other marsh and water birds. After the nesting season these gulls wander widely. The exodus from the Great Salt Lake region starts in late July. If the insect crop is good, one may see the gulls foraging about the high mountain lakes in Utah and in the Sierra Nevada in California. In late summer they are common from north of Monterey Bay to Oregon.

In my experience it has always been somewhat of a mystery where gulls spend their nights—winter or summer. In summer near Portland, Oregon, the western gulls sit on the sand flats in the Columbia River, gossiping or just looking at the passing boats during many daylight hours. My cruises up and down the river at night indicate they go elsewhere, possibly to the sloughs and lakes on Sauvies Island near the junction of the Columbia and Willamette Rivers. And yet, after sunrise they fly high over the city, coming up from the Columbia River in successive formations that consist of long V-shaped wavering lines. Often in mid-morning they return singly and in small groups to the sand flats for the siesta or gossip session.

In late summer evenings the gull parade going west over Lake Oswego, south of Portland, lasts for an hour. Some of these birds settle on the lake and paddle slowly out of the paths of slow-moving boats as late as 10:00 P.M. But the majority continue westward, going toward the sea. The Pacific Ocean, however, is seventy miles away. And when I drive to the coast and walk the beach at night, the gulls are not there. Probably the majority of these thousands of gulls seek rest on the river sand bars and islands, which are free from human intrusion during the darkest hours of the night.

In contrast with these relatively sedentary birds, the kittiwakes, which are graceful little gulls, range over the high seas for thousands of miles. They are the only gulls that remain beyond sight of land throughout the whole of the North Atlantic. Terns, which are in the same family (Laridae) with the gulls, are even greater travelers. Their long wings carry them over longer migratory routes than those undertaken by the gulls and they specialize on fish food to a greater extent than do the gulls. Much of their behavior, however, resembles that of the gulls, including their sociable nature.

Terneries, or breeding colonies, are on sand dunes, rocky shores, and grassy islands. The black tern constructs a floating nest in fresh-water marshes and lakes. The most fantastic nesting habit of all is practiced by the small, pure white, angel-like, fairy terns of the mid-Pacific atolls.

The female lays a single egg in a shallow depression on a bare branch of a tree or shrub. There she incubates the egg. When the youngster hatches, it clings securely to its branch through wind and rain and storm. The fairy tern is sometimes seen off the main Hawaiian islands.

The sooty tern, which ranges the tropical and subtropical seas, is noted for breeding on oceanic islands in such multitudes that from a distance its flocks resemble haze as they fly over their island colonies. Alexander Sprunt, Jr., in describing these birds on reefs off the west coast of Florida, speculated that Ponce de Leon must have seen them when he discovered the Dry Tortugas in the Gulf of Mexico in 1513. After more than four hundred years, the hovering, screaming swarms still nest on the Dry Tortugas each spring, now protected by the custodian of Fort Jefferson, which became a national monument in 1935.

The Arctic tern is the migration champion among terns. It breeds in Arctic America and migrates across the equator to the antarctic waters. Records of banded birds being recovered after flights of 10,000 to 14,000 miles are not unusual. Their travels remind us of jet-plane flights. Yet, in spite of being great sea travelers, terns are common inland in many states.

Caspian terns, for example, nest in the marshes near Great Salt Lake. Their numbers are small, possibly because gulls destroy many of their eggs. The least tern, which nests locally along the Pacific and Atlantic coasts and along inland rivers, occurs in the prairie states, and may be seen from Ohio southward to Louisiana and Texas. The common tern, a cosmopolitan bird, has been much studied on Cape Cod; 650,000 had been banded by the end of 1959.

These studies indicate that the same birds return to nest within a few feet of their previous nesting sites. Other studies have shown that gulls are enemies of terns and that the numbers of terns in some colonies fluctuate over a fifteen-year cycle as a result of gull predation. The greatest threat to tern survival now is the spread of DDT, which the birds acquire from minnows in marshes that have been sprayed for mosquito control.

The World of the Gull

Among the natural enemies of gulls are skuas and jaegers. These birds resemble gulls, but have darker plumages and different flight and feeding habits. Most of us will never see a skua. These large dark-brown birds are considered to be relatives of the gulls—they nest in the Arctic and range the North Atlantic (rarely to the North Pacific). The south polar skua breeds in colonies in Antarctica in close association with the Adelie penguins. During the nesting season their food consists almost entirely of penguin eggs, chicks, and dead adults. At other seasons they subsist on bird and animal carcasses exposed as the snow melts.

The skuas that breed in the Arctic are not numerous, and though they fly southward over the ocean they are rare along our coasts. Their feet

Southern skua. These birds of Antarctica, New Zealand, and the southern oceans attack gulls and terns and force them to give up food. They also eat eggs, young of other birds, small mammals, insects, and carrion. (Photo by E. Slater, C.S.I.R.O., Australia)

are webbed like those of gulls and are armed with claws. Their hooked bills and remarkable flight ability enable them to pursue gulls and other fishing birds and make them drop or even disgorge fish they have swallowed. The skuas (*Catharacta skua*, and subspecies) have attributes both of raptores and of gulls. They run and walk like gulls, but their flight is hawk-like. The strong hooked bill and the sharp curved claws enable them to fish for themselves or to live lives of pirates and predators. They pursue the smaller gulls with fury, they kill and eat kittiwakes and duck-lings, and they are sufficiently tyrannical to attack the golden eagle.

R. Meinertzhagen's book, *Pirates and Predators*, includes some colorful accounts of the depredations of skuas on various species of birds. (Incidentally, Meinertzhagen and other British authors also apply the name *skua* to jaegers (*Stercorarius*) as well). The skua forces ducks to dive until exhausted; when the duck surfaces the skua lands on the victim's back and hammers its skull. There is one record of a skua killing a heron in Shetland by striking it in the air and then continuing the attack in the water, pecking at the heron's head, and paddling with its feet to force its victim under water.

Skuas also kill gannets, black-backed gulls, and puffins. The skuas knock the puffins on the head as they bring fish to their nests in the ground. If the puffin slips into the hole unscathed, the skua waits above the hole and knocks the puffin out as it emerges. Small colonies of terns also are molested by skuas so that not a single chick survives. In larger colonies, combined attacks by terns succeed in beating off attacks. Meinertzhagen also reports that skuas follow ships in the North Atlantic, where they pick refuse off the sea; but more often, they wait until a gull has retrieved a morsel and then follow the gull until it disgorges.

Jaegers (pronounced yay'-gers) likewise are pirates of the air. Peter Freuchen and Finn Salomonsen, in their fascinating book *The Arctic Year*, state that kittiwakes and Arctic terns often are pursued by the parasitic jaeger, which obtains most of its food by aerial robbery. Dodging and other flight maneuvers are useless in the face of relentless pursuit by the jaeger, since it possesses superior flying skill and often is assisted by another jaeger. The food either is caught in the air or is picked up from the water. The victimized birds then have to return for another try at fishing.

According to Arthur Cleveland Bent, the parasitic jaeger is more of a gull robber than a predator and its actions in chasing gulls rarely result in bloodshed. It robs various species of terns, Bonaparte's gull, and kittiwakes. It hawks over the tundra for eggs of eiders and gulls and also eats shrews, mice, and lemmings. It can capture Lapland longspurs on the wing.

The pomarine jaeger, which is as large as a herring gull, nests across the continent in the Arctic. It is less aggressive than the parasitic jaeger, but it can pursue a tern or small gull and follow every twist and turn until the victim drops its fish. Bent writes: "Occasionally the indignant tern voids its excrement instead, which the jaeger immediately seizes, as if it were a dainty morsel."

The pomarine jaegers are summer and fall visitors to our coasts, where they may be seen harassing the smaller gulls, terns, and shearwaters. On

Left: parasitic jaeger chick, Kodiak Island, Alaska. (Photo by John Q. Hines)

Below: nest of the long-tailed jaeger. The eggs are spotted, as are gull eggs. (Photo by Alex Walker)

the Greenland coast they live principally on the labors of the kittiwakes. The pomarine jaegers are chased by smaller parasitic and long-tailed jaegers which are more adroit on the wing.

The long-tailed jaeger, which is somewhat larger than the parasitic jaeger, uses its broad tail effectively as a rudder as it pursues gulls or terns. Lemmings, however, constitute its principal food on its breeding grounds in the Arctic regions. Bent states that its pilfering of the eggs and young of other birds is done on the sly since gulls, terns, curlews, sandpipers, and other shore birds will attack and drive them away. They also seem to be more playful than other jaegers; six or eight may pursue one another back and forth over the marshy tundra.

Unlike the jaegers, gulls do not harass other birds by pursuing them on the wing. They are more likely to pursue their fellows, especially when a lucky bird obtains a choice morsel of food and is attempting to find a secluded spot where the food can be eaten in peace.

Gulls have excellent eyesight and are attracted by the activities of other gulls that have found food. They come close to investigate scraps of possible food material thrown from ships or piers. While crossing the Strait of Juan de Fuca, between Victoria, British Columbia, and Port Angeles, Washington, I have attracted gulls by throwing bits of bread on the water. But when I threw similar-sized bits of paper, they paid no attention.

Gulls communicate in many ways. Tinbergen (1960) lists calls, postures, and movements as forms of signaling behavior, which differs among the various species as a result of environmental influence on gull evolution. While on the ground, hostile postures include a loud call with the neck and body stretched at a 45-degree angle; this posture usually is directed at a distant flying gull. When an intruder is near, the neck is

Long-tailed jaeger, Kipnuk, Alaska. These birds force gulls to drop their food while on the wing. (Photo by Alex Walker)

Left: gull catching food tossed into the air. The feet act as rudders for quick maneuverability, and the wings are twisted for guidance.

Right: the winner puts on the brakes after catching a piece of meat thrown into the air.

stretched and the feathers lifted, while the bill points toward the ground.

Gulls express fear by standing side by side while looking away from one another. Some postures have become ritualized and possess special meanings. For example, hostility is shown by opening the mouth, and immature birds indicate appeasement when they keep their necks pulled in and hold their bodies close to the ground. Expressive postures and movements are also used in meeting ceremonies between the sexes, in begging for food from sexual partners, and in head tossing to stimulate mates to copulate.

When a gull rears upright and raises its wings, it is warning another of the consequences of intruding. If it pecks the ground or pulls grass or other objects with its bill, it is demonstrating what may happen to the visitor if a battle ensues. To avoid battle, the other gull may turn away, squat low, or even hide its head beneath a wing. Apparently the aggressor is forbidden to strike a bird that cannot see.

Food finding also involves a marvelous communication system. The next time you are at the seashore, toss some food scraps on the sand, start cleaning fish, or drop some of your lunch or fish bait from your boat and then time how long it takes the gulls to appear. Their amazing eyesight enables

Boat harbor and gulls on the Atlantic coast. (Photo by Dorothy B. Taylor)

them to interpret your movements as well as enabling them to locate a free meal.

Gulls of different species evolve various behavioral patterns useful in food finding. The black-headed gull and other species of gulls use the technique of walking backward in shallow pools and catching the animals disturbed by trampling. P. A. Buckley has reported foot-paddling, dancing, puddling, or treading for four American gulls: laughing gull, California gull, ring-billed gull, and Bonaparte's gull. Foot-paddling seems to be a common activity of laughing gulls. Jack P. Hailman found that his captive birds even foot-paddled on the cement floors of their cages.

Foot-paddling undoubtedly uncovers small vertebrates in shallow water. But the action sometimes suggests a dance, and it may be a ritualized behavior which probably evolved from experience. Bonaparte's gulls at the Jamaica Bay Wildlife Refuge, Long Island, New York, for example, were observed agitating water by rapid up-and-down movements of their feet. The birds, instead of feeding, however, turned their heads from side to side as if disinterested in the proceedings.

Basically foot-paddling may be a method of feeding, but its motivation is not entirely clear and it certainly is a controversial type of behavior. Ring-billed gulls have been observed to paddle for ten minutes at a time and a California gull paddled on the tidal flats in San Francisco Bay for fifteen minutes while looking down. A herring gull in Nova Scotia was seen making a trench by working backward. But both herring gulls and laughing gulls in Connecticut seemed to be indifferent to the results of their paddling.

Each species of gull has its own diet preference and its own method of obtaining food. Great black-backed gulls eat almost anything they can catch and kill, including rabbits, mice, and some of the smaller sea birds. In describing the feeding behavior of these large gulls, Alfred O. Gross cites the observations of several people who watched the gulls kill ducklings and adult birds, including the southern eider, the goldeneye, and the red-breasted merganser.

Gulls are guilty of various kinds of depredations. Meinertzhagen writes that the larger gulls nesting on a grouse moor may do more damage than all the ravens, crows, foxes, and stoats put together. He observed gulls pecking the eyes of new-born lambs. In Greenland he saw glaucous and Iceland gulls constantly on patrol for chicks and eggs in large fulmar colonies. Black-headed gulls have been seen mobbing coots, pirating various species of diving ducks, and even mobbing ravens, crows, and skuas.

Large gulls commonly nest in the vicinity of breeding colonies of smaller gulls and terns. This provides them with many opportunities for egg snatching. Arthur C. Twomey observed that California gulls swallowed eggs whole and carried them to the nesting colony. There the eggs were disgorged, broken, and eaten by adults and young. L. Ph. Bolander, Jr., once observed three California gulls and a glaucous-winged gull stealing worms from robins. The gulls waited until the robins were pulling worms and then charged to make them let go of their prey.

The extensive travels of gulls around their summer colonies result in exploration of many hundreds of square miles. Gull travels and gull co-operativeness make starvation almost unknown in the gull world. Their numbers and their attributes for food finding are assurance that some-where they will find carrion, fishes, shrimps, dead birds, rodents, eggs, fruit, maggots, germinating wheat, worms, chicken heads, garbage, barnacles, clams, grasshoppers, or whatever the country affords, even if nothing more than pieces of bone. Through the gull's eyes, nature is bountiful indeed.

Nature is also cruel to gulls. As pointed out previously, they are rapa-cious birds and notorious killers of their own young and those of their neighbors. They also have other enemies. Even the large herring gulls

Grasshoppers are food for multitudes of inland gulls.

distrust peregrines and eagles. Crows and ravens likewise are gull enemies, since these birds are accomplished thieves of eggs and chicks.

As Behle points out, one might expect gulls to harbor numerous harmful parasites obtained from their scavenger diet, but they seem to be singularly free of parasitic worms and diseases. Tapeworms have been found in gulls, which are also susceptible to deadly botulism, a form of food-poisoning, which afflicts ducks in large numbers.

Snakes are probably infrequent enemies of gulls, but they may be predators in gull colonies near lakes. Behle on July 29, 1941, on Antelope Island, Utah, saw a gopher snake apparently squeezing a two-week-old gull to death. The snake released the gull upon being disturbed, but swallowed a chick taken from a pipped egg. More recently, A. W. Champagne sent me a picture taken by the Nevada Game Commission of a gopher snake near a gull nest on Anaho Island in Pyramid Lake. The photographer disturbed the snake, which was ready to engulf the gull eggs.

Mammal predators of gulls are numerous. Foxes prey on gull eggs and young. Stoats and hedgehogs are a threat to the broods of black-headed gulls in England. Gull colonies on islands are relatively safe from mammal predation, but inland colonies are always subject to the depredations of coyotes, weasels, skunks, and rats.

Although gulls, to a certain extent, are birds of the storms, weather is occasionally a major cause of death. When waves are roughened by high winds and tides are high, gulls of the seacoast have difficulty in seeing and catching their prey. The chicks in their nest are exposed to lower temperatures and inadequate food supplies. Then they weaken and die.

Gulls raised on inland breeding grounds encounter summer hazards when storms inundate their colonies and the chicks drown in rain pools. Young gulls also wander from their nests to seek shelter from wind and rain and become lost or die because the parents are not able to find and brood them.

Although young gulls seek shade and avoid the summer sun, they have a relatively great capacity for internal temperature regulation. This enables them to withstand the intense heat from the sun's rays. George A. Bartholomew, Jr., and William R. Dawson found that western gull chicks in rookeries at the north end of Angel de la Guarda, a desert island located in the Gulf of California, endured direct sunlight for as long as an hour without apparent ill effects. Naked young pelicans in the same locality depended on being shaded by the adults, which were very attentive.

The young gulls when heated breathed rapidly through their open mouths. Gull chicks in the sun had temperatures about 2° C. higher than those in the shade. Their ability to dissipate heat is derived largely from panting, which results in evaporative cooling from the moist lining membranes of the respiratory tract. Birds do not have sweat glands but can lose some heat by vaporization of moisture from the skin.

Once past the crucial weeks as chicks, the newly feathered gulls learn to seek shelter from heat or cold, depending on where they live. Then their life expectancy becomes fairly high. With the waning of summer they are ready for the great adventures of exploring, hunting, migrating, and flocking together in places far from the land of their birth.

Franklin's gull in breeding plumage. Malheur National Wildlife Refuge, Oregon.

Autumn

THE RESTLESSNESS of autumn comes early for the gulls. During my years along the Oregon and Washington coasts I always looked forward to sightings of jaegers, terns, and gulls. The general flight of California gulls

Gulls show their intelligence by their awareness of what is happening around them.

appeared as early as July or August. Then as the youngsters of other species became air-borne they came in increasing numbers in late August and early September. When the goldenrods were in yellow glory and the vine maples in the fir forests were violently crimson, then the migrating flocks of gulls were at their best.

Autumn fishing trips along the coast frequently gave me the opportunity to see Bonaparte's gulls. These tree-nesting gulls come down from the northern interior of British Columbia and appear among the San Juan Islands in northern Puget Sound still in their summer plumage. The adults have black heads that later change to white. The immature birds are easily distinguished by the black tail-band which disappears when they molt to the adult plumage. Fall fishermen welcome these gulls, which feed on small herrings pushed to the surface of the sea by feeding coho salmon. The flocks of diving gulls are nature's best indicator of the location of schools of fish.

Ring-billed gulls come down the Columbia River from interior breeding grounds and are common from October on through the winter. They meet the mew gulls also coming south from their nesting grounds in Alaska. These are joined by the Heermann's gulls coming north from their nesting sites along the coast of Mexico. Together with the resident western gulls and glaucous-winged gulls, more than a dozen other species of gulls appear along the Oregon coast.

Coastal migrations are not the only travels made by gulls. The pelagic gulls, such as the kittiwakes, are not greatly affected by storms and remain well scattered off shore. Inland, the great movement of California gulls begins with the migration of young birds toward the Pacific coast. In September 1969, more than thirty thousand immature California gulls

Gulls coming in for a landing.

were seen near the mouth of the Columbia River. Most of these were birds of the year. Many had been banded near Laramie, Wyoming.

Autumn also is the time for great migrations of gulls along the eastern coast of North America. The laughing gulls, which breed from Nova Scotia to Florida and the Gulf of Mexico, make coastwise journeys that take some of the northern birds to the coast of South Carolina and the southern birds to the coast of South America. The herring gulls move southward to winter all the way from southern Alaska to most of the United States. Many of those reared on inland lakes, however, remain within a few hundred miles of their colonies. Banding studies of herring gulls on islands in Lake Erie and Lake Huron indicate that most of the adults remain near home. But some of the young birds wander as far south as Mexico and the West Indies.

In contrast with the gulls that most of us know, some of the arctic gulls do not come south to our latitudes at all. Peter Freuchen and Finn Salomonsen report that the ivory gulls in October follow the border zone of the drift ice to eastern Greenland and Baffin Bay. They do not approach land unless heavy gales drive them in close to the coast. Ross's gulls start in September and October a strange eastward migration that takes them from the continental shelf of Siberia across northern Alaska. After they pass Point Barrow and fly in a northeastern direction toward the Beaufort Sea, they disappear, probably to winter in the complete darkness of the icy waste near the North Pole.

The glaucous gulls usually migrate southward, but the final stragglers vacate the high arctic regions only after the ice cover is complete in October. They go only far enough to find open water along the coast or among the islands. A few casual visitors come as far south as California and the Great Lakes. Infrequently one is observed as a rare winter resident in Colorado.

Gulls in autumn are great pedestrians. Wherever one sees them—in saline marshes, or dunes, river banks, ponds, ocean beaches—they walk slowly, searching for insects, dead birds, fishes, or other food items to

Left: gulls on take-off can lift directly into the air. If the wind is calm and they are not frightened, they use the beach or other level area as a runway before becoming air-borne.

Right: gull-watching is one of the pleasures of sea voyages.

satisfy their omnivorous appetites. They do not need to retreat from high seas, winds, snow or ice, and so they walk. Often I have seen them walking on lawns in school grounds, in parks, and in the fields where farmers were digging carrots or harvesting cabbages and pumpkins.

The large species of gulls are addicted to perching on buildings, telephone poles, and pilings. From these vantage points they watch for refuse in the streets, in harbors, and around fishing boats. When they are air-borne, they poise with elegant ease over ferryboats. Sometimes they circle in the sky for what appears to be exercise or pure pleasure. When the winds are right, they form long processions around headlands, rise to great heights, and sail downwind, only to repeat the long procession. This continuous parade allows no morsel of food to escape their notice.

Feeding methods differ among gull species. The mew gulls and Bonaparte's gulls flutter over the water with dangling feet and pick up in their bills floating particles or small fish. Western gulls and herring gulls are not averse to flying out over the open ocean to splash down and scoop up herring, smelt, and other small fishes that appear in schools. Gulls, however, are not skilled in diving, as are the pelicans, cormorants, gannets, murres, and puffins. But Heermann's gulls sometimes rob the brown pelicans by snatching a fish from their bills as they surface after a deep plunge.

In autumn some of the small gulls such as Bonaparte's gull and Franklin's gull spend considerable time on the wing catching insects in the air. Larger gulls, such as the herring gulls in the Lake States, find good hunting in the fields where the seasonal crop of grasshoppers has

Ground squirrels and other rodents are caught and eaten by gulls.

matured. I have also seen them scavenging dead rodents and rabbits along the highways in North Dakota and Minnesota in late September.

In view of the omnivorous diet of the gulls, it is not surprising that a considerable amount of the food they eat is of vegetable origin. Organic refuse, meat, insects, eggs, and other animal life constitute their normal food. But in autumn, when eggs and the young of ducks, avocets, gulls, and other birds are not available, they turn readily to a variety of plant foods. Most species of gulls apparently have this adaptability, whether they live in the Arctic, in moderate climates, or in the tropics.

Gulls of different species associate with one another in feeding and resting areas. Usually each species has its separate nesting ground.

As already mentioned, California gulls frequently present a problem to cherry growers. Franklin's gulls in the prairie states sometimes feed upon wheat, oats, and other grains. Herring gulls of the Maine coast cause damage to the blueberry crop and ring-billed gulls in Oregon eat the seeds of various native grasses. Glaucous gulls in Greenland eat kelp and other algae.

In a report on California gull food habits, Clyde R. Odin found that "seeds of muskmelon, watermelon, smartweed, cherry, pigweed, and wheat and rye were found in 12.2 percent of the stomachs examined." In the autumn of 1969 I saw California gulls eating the seeds from pumpkins that had been crushed during harvest near the end of the runway at Portland International Airport.

The meat-eating habits of gulls bring them into direct conflict with many species of birds and other animals. Gull predation on nesting colonies of ducks, terns, and other water birds occasionally is decidedly harmful. On the other hand, when a gull snatches a fish from the gular pouch of a pelican, the action is a nuisance but not overly detrimental to pelican existence.

The list of bird species subject to gull predation is extensive: Canada goose, common mallard, cinnamon teal, pintail, redhead, pheasant, avocet, American coot, long-billed curlew, red-winged blackbird, and gulls of various species. Egg-robbing by gulls is more intense when colonies become overcrowded and food shortages become critical.

Predation by gulls sometimes results in great population changes among sea birds. At the beginning of the present century, for example, lessening of human interference and subsequent protection of bird colonies on the Maine coast resulted in competition between herring gulls and terns. Ultimately the terns were driven out and then great black-backed gulls began to encroach on herring gull colonies. This type of menace has developed in many other places such as Tern Island at Chatham, Massachusetts, where common and roseate terns were driven away by herring gulls in 1964.

79

Cormorants and gull in the harbor at Stanley, British Columbia.

Difficulties between colonial nesting birds are minimized when the nesting grounds are far apart. But the aggressiveness of gulls accentuates the difficulties of other species of birds in raising their young even when the gulls do not nest in the same colonies with larger neighbors. Behle states that California gulls are more dominant than cormorants, herons, or pelicans that nest in proximity on the islands in Great Salt Lake. The herons are watchful birds and faithfully guard their nests, even though they appear to be unsociable among themselves. The pelicans and cormorants each act like family groups and thus nest and rest in close proximity. The pelicans suffer most, since the gull colonies are usually in closest contact with them. Human visitors are most inimical to the large birds, which leave their nests while the bolder gulls remain and use the opportunity to break and eat the eggs of the other birds.

Man has always been one of the greatest enemies of gulls. Kittiwakes formerly were victims of men; Bent notes that "in winter, when these gulls are abundant on the New England coast, they are shot in large numbers. They are tame and unsuspicious, gathering, like terns, in large flocks over a fallen companion, making it easy for the gunner to kill as many as he chooses." Bent also quotes William Macgillivray, who wrote in 1852 that he had seen ". . . a person station himself on top of the kittiwake cliff of the Isle of May, and shoot incessantly for several hours, without so much as afterwards picking up a single individual of the many killed and maimed birds with which the smooth water was strewn beneath."

White pelican breeding ground, Tule Lake, California. Pelicans carefully guard their nests to protect them from gull raids. (Oregon Game Commission photo)

The World of the Gull

I have seen frustrated duck hunters shoot gulls around irrigation reservoirs in northeastern Colorado. Gull eggs used to be collected in thousands for sale in eastern and western markets. Persistent egging on the Farallones once greatly reduced the population of western gulls, but the practice has long since been stopped.

The Eskimos have long known that the breasts of glaucous and other gulls are desirable as food. Besides shooting the gulls, they use spears and bows and arrows to capture them. Some Eskimos use baited lines with hooks or pointed sticks.

Foxes and bobcats occasionally catch adult gulls while they are roosting at night on beaches or sand dunes. Kay Snow, who lives in Portland, Oregon, recently told me that she saw a sea lion dunk a gull several times near Three Arch Rocks west of Oceanside, Oregon. The bedraggled gull ultimately escaped.

There is considerable information about gulls and other sea birds that have been caught, attacked, and even swallowed by the angler fish, monk fish, and sharks. John K. Terres, in his book *Flashing Wings*, reports that several years ago duck hunters on Raritan Bay, New Jersey, saw an angler fish struggling on the surface, apparently unable to sink. On being hoisted into the boat, the fish was found to have a large herring gull stuck in its throat. Apparently the fish had caught the gull while it was asleep, for its head was still tucked in back of one wing. Terres also notes that the angler fish attacks gulls, loons, and other waterbirds, and that fishermen

Nest of California gull.

have seen the 8-foot-long monk fish whisk cormorants below the surface with incredible speed.

A seemingly unlikely predator of gulls is the octopus. However, several instances of bird attacks by these cephalopods have been reported by K. A. Hindwood. In February, 1956, a boating party at Eaglehawk Neck, Tasmania, released a silver gull that was held by a small octopus with a tentacle about each wing of the struggling bird. Another silver gull was found in the grip of an octopus at Long Reef, near Sydney, Australia. The octopus, concealed under a low rock shelf, had held the gull by one of its legs obviously for a considerable time, for the bird was weak when released. Hindwood also reported octopuses' catching crested terns and fairy penguins.

Gulls seem to be afflicted with few diseases. Carlton M. Herman and Gordon Bolander, however, found in the San Francisco Bay area a glaucous-winged gull dead of a disease caused by the fungus, *Aspergillus fumigatus*. This disease causes mycotic pneumonia in wild and domestic birds, and has also been reported in herring gulls around the harbor of Boston, Massachusetts.

Diseases, shooting, and predation have not caused major changes in gull populations. Instead, great shifts in gull numbers have resulted from indirect influences of man's activities in disturbing the face of the earth. The draining of prairie lakes and ponds, filling of estuaries, pollution of waters resulting in decimation of fishes and other gull food, oil spills along the coasts, drainage of Gulf Coast swamps formerly used by gulls in autumn and winter, and flooding of rivers and bays with untreated sewage that kills fish have decreased gull populations in some localities and have caused them to migrate to other places, where they have increased.

Herring gulls were rare birds along the New England coast in the latter part of the nineteenth century. The eggs and young were used for human food and a set of adult wings was worth forty cents in the millinery trade. But in the 1890's, wardens of the National Audubon Society were hired to guard some of the breeding colonies off the Maine coast. Human use of

Gulls are interested in people who feed them regularly.

eggs and gull wings decreased in succeeding years, and an international treaty for protection of migratory birds was signed in 1916. The growth of gull breeding colonies and southward migration to Massachusetts and New York then increased, until the gulls became a nuisance and the U.S. Fish and Wildlife Service contracted for control methods, which consisted mainly of destruction of their eggs by spraying them with oil and formaldehyde. Since the early 1900's, however, John A. Kadlec and William H. Drury have concluded after extensive study that the herring gull breeding population in New England has been doubling every twelve to fifteen years.

These recent increases in gull breeding populations have resulted in increased autumn migrations, so that herring gulls now are familiar birds along our southern coasts. Protection has made gulls so tame that many species now scavenge among the bathers on Florida and California coasts. Many of these are young gulls, which have a tendency to wander farther from their breeding grounds than do breeding adults.

Autumn gulls show a confusing array of plumages. The second molt, which produces the first winter plumage, results in brown herring gulls with black bills. Molts in succeeding years make the birds lighter and lighter until in their third year their white heads, gray mantles, and flesh-colored bills mark them as full adults. The brown eyes of youngsters also change to yellow as the heads change to white with maturity.

During my years in the Northwest, I always looked forward to autumn as an exciting time for study and identification of the migrating gulls. The plumages were new and many of the gulls foraged together, so that size comparisons could be made as an aid to recognition of the different

Gull tracks in the sand.

species. The mew gulls, for example, are smaller than the California gulls and ring-billed gulls. In turn, the California gulls are smaller than herring gulls, and they also have greenish instead of flesh-colored legs.

Autumn gull-watching calls for sharp eyes in observing other bird features, including the subtle nuances of mantle tones. The dark-gray mantle of the western gull is different from the pearly-gray mantle of the herring gull, if you view them in the right light. Also, the faces of young western gulls are darker than those of the herring gulls. But when the two species are not standing side by side, how dark is dark, or how light is light? In the absence of side-by-side comparison, one must look for other characteristics, such as general appearance, amount of white on the wing tips, or the blackness of the wing tips themselves. But then you have to remember that the wing tips of glaucous and glaucous-winged gulls are never black. In this respect the Audubon Bird guides by Richard Pough, the Peterson Field guides, and the Golden Press paperback *Birds of North America* by Chandler S. Robbins *et al.*, can be of great help in the identification of gulls.

All these plumage variations apparently present few problems to experienced observers, although I have seen them change their opinions when the gull was in hand. But I am willing to be called a novice at field identification. Just being afield with the gulls as they arrive in autumn is an adventure that is always new.

Winter

THE WINTER RESORTS of the gulls are almost as varied as the numbers of
species of gulls. When winter comes, gulls do not necessarily attempt to
escape cold weather, since they have downy inner feathers that insulate
them against sleet, snow, and cold even in subarctic climates. Being opportunistic birds, they seek winter quarters where food can be found.

A few species, like the black-legged kittiwake, leave their arctic breeding

Gulls sometimes preen, rest, or sleep for hours on mild winter days.

grounds and spread far and wide over the oceans in wintertime. These children of the winds and waves have no need to come to land, since the ocean supplies their food.

Some of the arctic and antarctic gulls endure what to us seems to be the most horrible climate in the world. The ivory gulls, for example, move southward in October to the east coast of Greenland, or to Baffin Bay and Davis Strait. They remain at the edge of the drift ice and do not come to land unless driven by heavy storms. In the arctic darkness the ivory gulls eat whatever remnants of dead fishes, crustaceans, and mammal carrion they can find. Ross's gulls live in an even more extraordinary bird world; they apparently winter in darkness where they find open water in the pack ice of the polar sea.

Other hardy arctic gulls, such as the glaucous gull, follow the coast

Snowy owls live in the Arctic and are enemies of young gulls. (Oregon Game Commission photo)

lines southward but stop their migrations where open water remains at the edge of the drift ice. The great black-backed gulls now are winter residents southward to New Jersey and South Carolina; and immatures have been reported to the Florida Keys.

In contrast with the coastal southward movement of many gulls, Franklin's gulls make the long flight from the prairie regions to the Gulf of Mexico or to their main winter quarters on the western coast of South America, even as far south as Patagonia. By this migration to and from the Southern Hemisphere, they essentially live in summer, or at least in mild weather, the year around. The dusky gull, however, beats them at this game. It wanders only among the Galapagos Islands and thus lives perpetually in an equatorial climate.

The gulls most of us see in the United States in winter are birds that

Arctic foxes eat gull eggs and chicks. These pure white animals blend with the ice and snow in the Arctic night. (Photo by Colin McDonald)

have dispersed from their breeding grounds instead of moving long distances from northern or southern summer homes. The herring gulls of the Atlantic coast and the California gulls of the Pacific coast wander from one place to another searching for food in their wintering areas. For them, finding food is more important than attachment to any given locality.

California gulls and ring-billed gulls in the winter of 1957 left their regular territory along the Pacific coast and congregated in great numbers in eastern Oregon, where one of the most severe irruptions of meadow voles ever recorded reached numbers of more than two thousand per acre.

Gulls are not afraid of human habitation or construction projects if food is nearby.

Winter

Along with disease, decreasing rodent food, weather factors, and metabolic disturbances, predation by mammals, hawks, and gulls brought the vole population back to normal proportions. Thus, as transient predators, the gulls helped relieve the land of one of nature's plagues.

Living prey is usually at low ebb in winter, so the adaptable gulls specialize in scavenging. At city garbage dumps they sometimes wait in fantastic numbers for each truck load of refuse. At the dump near Portland, Oregon, the gulls sit so tightly packed that the garbage men amuse themselves by rushing into the mob and catching gulls that get tangled in the mighty confusion of beating wings.

Gulls swarm at the garbage dump.

The World of the Gull

When a load of garbage is dumped, the screaming mob of fighting birds obscures the refuse pile until the clamorous group has sorted out the edible scraps of food. Similarly, at Depot Bay, Oregon, the scramble for fish entrails when salmon are cleaned at the docks results in bedlam above and in the water of the bay. When the feast is done, the gulls sit quietly on buildings or walk sedately on the beach looking for sea worms, clams, and dead fish.

Although food gathering in winter presents occasional problems for gulls, weather gives them little inconvenience even in northern latitudes. The heavy rainstorms of the Pacific Northwest apparently go unnoticed by the western gulls, ring-billed gulls, and mew gulls that congregate in

Iceberg in the Arctic world of the gull.

flooded pastures to dissect matted grass and turn over debris in search of grubs and worms.

The arctic gulls endure snow and cold apparently without discomfort. In the polar whiteness, heat conservation is all-important. Body warmth is maintained by the thick plumage and by the cells of air in the white feathers, which reduce heat conduction.

Behavioral characteristics also protect gulls, especially those that live in the barren ice fields of the far north. Peter Freuchen and Finn Salomonsen in *The Arctic Year* note that the ivory gulls wade in shallow water in search of food but rise into the air as soon as the water reaches their belly feathers. They suggest that this avoids the risk that the water on the feathers may freeze them to an ice crust. Ivory gulls also display no fear of feeding bears or of men working at whaling or sealing stations.

In the more moderate climate of the United States, many gulls remain throughout the winter. Even when the bays, lakes, and rivers freeze over in our northern states, gulls can be seen sitting on the ice. If the ice is thick enough for men to fish through, gulls frequent the vicinity to retrieve small fishes, water dogs (salamanders, used for bait), and sandwich scraps thrown away by the fishermen.

Gull populations do fluctuate in the North in winter. Their numbers increase on the Great Lakes when lakes farther north are closed by ice. In

Gull cruising the beach at low tide looking for food left by human visitors.

January, during mild weather, I have seen many California gulls on the irrigation reservoirs in Colorado and on the lake near the zoo in Denver. Snow storms and blizzards drive them away and sometimes they do not return for many weeks.

Gulls that winter along the Atlantic, Pacific, and Gulf Coasts always have access to water and sandy beaches where finding food is not a serious problem. The coastal gulls seem to do a great deal of local traveling. Niko Tinbergen (1967) observed that the herring gulls along the Dutch coast constantly fly along the dunes, sometimes in streams from opposite directions. They make these local excursions in search of food when the beach is covered by a combination of high tide and in-shore winds. The gulls also sail for hours, with scarcely a wing-beat, when the winds are strong and the upcurrents are pronounced over the irregular dunes.

Storms are often helpful to gulls. In windy weather food from the sea is cast up by the waves and the birds find it easily as they glide in the gale with effortless ease. Upcurrents around rocky islands, along high ridges, and over hilly terrain at the oceanside enable the gulls to soar, glide, and circle in what sometimes appears to be sport or the pure joy of flying.

The flight of gulls varies greatly, depending on the weather, the time of day, and the behavior routine determined by hunger, the presence of enemies, and the needs of young gulls on the nest. In windy weather the graceful flight of the gull always excites the admiration of human observers and at the same time seems shrouded in mystery.

Through the years various explanations have been offered for this seemingly mysterious feat of gliding on almost motionless wings. Actually, the aerodynamics of bird flight is similar to that of an airplane's wing, as John K. Terres has nicely described it in his book *Flashing Wings*. The gull is naturally designed to take advantage of *lift* resulting from air-pressure differences below and above its wings. Also, it is streamlined so that *drag* that tends to hold the bird back is minimized. In addition, the bird has "propellers" (primary feathers of the wings), which can be varied in pitch by twisting the wing tips while the wings beat. A living and

The long primary wing feathers, or flight feathers, are used as "propellers" and the inner part of the wings supports the gull in leisure flight. In rapid flight the whole wing gives propulsion and supports the bird.

sensitive organism, the gull automatically makes whatever adjustments are necessary to take advantage of air currents that provide pathways for gliding.

Gulls ride rising air currents over hills, promontories, and over warm water, which heats the air so that it ascends in vertical columns. Gulls are particularly well acquainted with the rising currents created by winds striking the sides of ships. When the wind is low, they also glide near the surface of the sea by using the local air currents that bounce from waves.

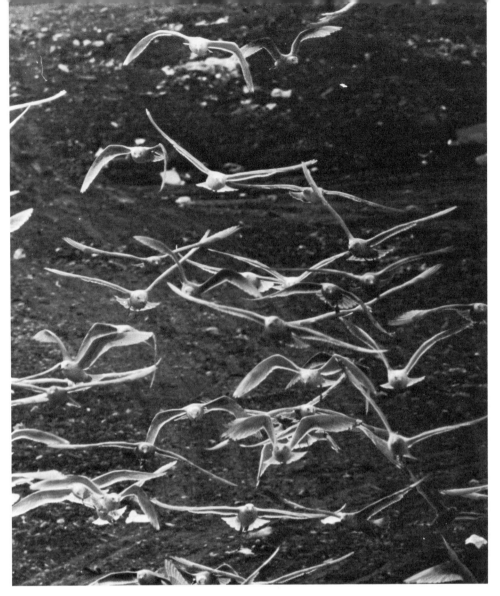

Gulls are gregarious creatures even in flight. Note the wingspread and the streamlined bodies.

When the wind is calm, as in cities in early morning, large gulls flap with broad wing beats—about two per second. On the way to their feeding grounds, they fly in long tapering lines and not infrequently in V formations like those used by ducks and geese. When the wind is calm, these flight formations improve aerodynamic efficiency.

In a recent analysis of bird flight formation, P. B. S. Lissaman and Carl A. Schollenberger present evidence that the power savings in V flight can result in 71 percent more flight distance than the range attainable by a lone bird. Unlike a fixed-wing airplane, birds can sense optimal formations. The advantages of flight formation are even greater when there is a tail wind.

The gull habit of soaring upward in flocks is not just for exercise. It places the gulls in position to see other gulls and the food-producing activities of human and other agencies for many miles. John K. Terres, in his book on bird flight, cites the calculations of Colonel Richard Meinertzhagen that on a clear day the visible horizon is 27 miles away from a bird flying 500 feet above the ground and 39 miles for a bird flying at 1,000 feet.

This explains to me how the Franklin's gulls readily find within the hour farming activities where insects and worms are being disturbed and

Resting period for ring-billed gulls, mew gulls, and glaucous-winged gulls on a winter day in the Pacific Northwest. As they stand or sit, they face into the wind.

made available for capture. On July 9, 1970, for example, at approximately 9:00 A.M., I saw five flocks of Franklin's gulls in different fields between Fort Collins and Loveland, Colorado, feeding behind plows or in alfalfa fields where cutting had just been started. Undoubtedly the gulls had located these activities from great heights and their swift flight had brought them quickly to an abundant source of food.

In winter the daily flights of gulls are made directly and primarily between their feeding and sleeping grounds. They usually rest on open flats, beaches, sandy river shores, or quiet lakes. When winds are high and the waters are turbulent, they seek sheltered land areas where wide expanse of territory enables them to see approaching predators.

The pedestrian gull. Unlike most birds, gulls walk, swim, and fly with ease.

Winter

On warm winter days the social resting grounds of gulls are sites for peaceful gatherings in the sun. Hundreds of gulls stand silently side by side or sit quietly on the ground. If the wind is blowing, they sit facing in the direction from which it comes. In the multitude a few pedestrian gulls wander from place to place and get pecked if they come too close to adults that have high standing in the gull hierarchy.

Sometimes the gulls tarry for hours in flocks on ice-covered lakes. Always, however, individuals or small groups come and go all day. If these wanderers discover food, the word somehow is passed along and the large group quickly deserts the resting ground.

Night roosts of the gulls are not permanent stands maintained throughout the winter. I have seen the glaucous-winged gulls sleeping for several nights in succession on the water at night on Lake Oswego, near Portland, Oregon, in groups of a hundred or more. Then suddenly they are gone, probably to rest on the Columbia River sandy islands where they are free from human interference. Many of them fly to the large fresh-water lakes in the slough where the Willamette River flows into the Columbia. In stormy weather some of the gulls fly to the Pacific Ocean some seventy miles away. Daily round-trip flights of fifty to one hundred miles or more are not unusual for these birds.

Kees Vermeer found that color-banded adult glaucous-winged gulls traveled a distance of approximately forty-five miles between their resting ground on Mandarte Island and their feeding area in Vancouver, British Columbia. He observed a mated pair of these gulls that occupied and defended a winter territory on the island. He observed that "when both were present, they often were approximately 2 feet apart."

Other observers have noted that pairing is part of the winter behavior of gulls. Herring gull pairs, according to Tinbergen (1953), do not show personal attachment such as can be observed during the mating season. And the bond can be broken by the appearance of a new mate in late winter or early spring. Boundary clashes between different pairs are not common in winter, since the nesting territory usually is not yet established.

99

The World of the Gull

On warm days in winter, gulls have their lackadaisical moments or hours. When one wants to see them in action they can sometimes be exasperating by their lack of activity. I once watched a western gull while it sat for three hours on a piling at the fishing wharf at Garibaldi, Oregon. Once it scratched its bill with its left foot. Twice it shifted its direction so its head pointed into the wind. And once it stood erect when a fisherman bumped his boat against the dock and shook the gull's perching post. Otherwise, it neither preened its feathers, reacted to other gulls flying overhead, nor gave evidence of hunger. If it slept, it did so with its eyes open.

The behavioral activities of gulls in winter, while divided mainly between flying, feeding, resting, preening, and avoiding danger, demonstrate a remarkable variety of specializations and adaptations as well as limitations in mental capacity. I once watched a western gull peck periodically for three days at the carcass of a seal on the beach at Oceanside, Oregon. The bird was at least persistent. But it never penetrated the hide of the dead seal and apparently was incapable of recognizing that it was wasting its energy.

At this same beach the glaucous-winged gulls quickly learned that the arm-waving signal of my friend Mr. Winston H. Taylor meant that feeding time had arrived. He merely had to walk from his house to the edge of the bluff above the sea and move his arm as though he were tossing bread into the air. Within minutes the gulls would appear and catch tidbits while flying or voraciously eat the meat scraps placed on a table in front of his house. In his absence, and at the same hour of the day, I tried to attract the gulls with the motion of tossing food into the air. But the gulls never came. I can only believe that they recognized him as an individual and a friend.

Although ring-billed and western gulls were present on this beach, they never came for the food offered by Mr. Taylor. One might assume that these species did not respond to the signals or that they were cautious because of fear of man. On their resting grounds, however, these three species of gulls associate harmoniously with one another.

Size differences between gulls of different species do result in competition when food is scarce. Arthur Cleveland Bent quotes an account by W. L. Dawson, who observed that mew gulls, which associate with glaucous-winged, herring, and Bonaparte's gulls on the coast of Washington in winter, are not fitted for competition with their larger associates. Their bills are small and they cannot scream and trumpet like the glaucous-winged gulls. Being more timid, they rest on the water while the big gulls stand on wharves and buildings ready to snatch food when it appears from any source.

Competition between different gull species is lessened by different preferences for wintering grounds and territories. The herring gulls so common along the north Atlantic coast do not compete with the laughing

Young western gull attempting to strip flesh from a dead seal on the Oregon coast.

gulls, which prefer warm-water regions far to the south. Herring gulls flock inland to feeding grounds and roosting places, whereas the ring-billed gulls prefer the tidal areas and the edge of the sea, where they follow in the wakes of ships.

Gulls from a given colony travel to different feeding grounds. This reduces the number of birds that depend on the limited food supply in any given area. When pressure on food supplies is critical, some gulls begin their migrations earlier than usual.

The dates of departure from wintering grounds thus vary widely even among gulls of the same species. Numbers of glaucous-winged gulls around

Gull food is exposed by the outgoing tide.

Winter

Seattle, Washington, and Vancouver, British Columbia, increase rapidly after February. California gulls return to the Great Salt Lake region in late February and early March. At first they arrive in small flocks, then in larger flocks, and the final stragglers appear in early June. Heermann's gulls, after wintering as far north as Puget Sound, reverse the usual migration route and gradually move south to their breeding grounds along the coasts of Lower California and Mexico.

The northward migration of the herring gulls and other species common

Drift ice in the Arctic where the glaucous, ivory, and Iceland gulls spend much of their lives. (Photo by Colin McDonald)

on the Atlantic coast and in subarctic regions is a leisurely affair. Individuals and small groups advance as the snow disappears and retreat when adverse weather returns and closes the rivers and lagoons. Many gulls wander northward as the ice channels open and the tundra becomes free of ice. Other thousands hardly migrate at all, since their winter and summer ranges are geographically the same.

It is always a pleasure to see the gulls as spring approaches. They seem to be more active than usual and their far-reaching cries are harbingers of pleasant days ahead. Also, their new plumages are neat and bright.

The glaucous-winged gull adults, for example, are white-headed in late February or March. The molt of the head, neck, and breast has released the dark feathers of the previous fall and early winter. Even the red spot on the lower mandible is bright and clear in readiness for the instinctive bill pecking by the newly hatched chicks.

The yellow bills and red spots of the California gulls also are intensified in color. The tails of the mature birds now are pure white. And the Bonaparte's gulls that were characterized by grayish white on the autumn migration now appear with black heads.

All other species of gulls show variations in the pattern of plumage and in their increasing sociability as the time comes for return to the breeding colonies. Once more the great assemblages of water birds begin the cycle of raucous activity that culminates in courtship, nest building, hatching of downy young, hunting, thieving, scavenging, and sorting out a new generation of long-winged, opportunistic birds familiar to people throughout the world.

Gulls and Men

GULLS AND MEN have been involved with one another through most of recorded history. In Deuteronomy 14:12-19, we read that unclean things not to be eaten are eagles, vultures, storks, cormorants, and gulls. Surely old Glaucus, the mythological fisherman of Boeotia, who later became a sea-god, knew the gulls, including possibly the glaucous gull itself. Certainly Columbus, sailing westward in October 1492, saw gulls among the migrating birds that crossed his course toward a new land.

When Cortez, the Spanish adventurer, landed 16 head of horses in the vicinity of Vera Cruz on the eastern coast of Mexico in 1515, he must have seen gulls. When Coronado left the little town of Compostello on the west coast of Mexico on February 23, 1540, on his exploration to the northeast, he probably saw gulls there in winter residence. But these explorers, the first settlers at Jamestown, and other Europeans who gained early footholds on the new continent were too busy establishing grazing animals, developing settlements, and invading the wilderness to record their sightings of gulls.

Nevertheless, early explorers in America saw gulls. Giovanni da Verrazano, an Italian navigator, sent in 1523 by Francis I, king of France, to find a passage to the East, made a landfall near Cape Fear, North Carolina, and then sailed north around Cape Hatteras, Narragansett Bay,

105

and Cape Cod to Cape Breton Island. He saw the cliffs and islands of the Gaspé Peninsula covered with murres, guillemots, and gulls.

In his intrepid exploration along the St. Lawrence in 1534, Jacques Cartier, the Frenchman, and his sailors saw sea birds in such numbers that "all the ships of France might load a cargo of them." The great auks, large as geese and with wings too small to fly, sat among the rocks or swam in thousands along the shore. The Frenchmen slaughtered them with clubs and salted them down in casks. They did not kill the gannets, ducks, geese, and gulls that swarmed over the islands and filled the air with their incredible numbers.

From these early times to the present the history of man-and-gull relationships has been one of gull watching, gull classification, gull pro-

Suppertime. The gulls come regularly for food at this table in Oceanside, Oregon.

tection by unnumbered human friends, and gull persecution by men who have created the very conditions that enabled the gulls to become local nuisances.

Before white men came to our shores, and throughout the early years of our modern society, gulls maintained their populations in balance with their enemies and their natural food supplies. But in the last hundred years or so we have encroached upon nature, decimated the land, and polluted our waters. Each year some of our wildlife species have dwindled. But the gulls have thrived on our ever-increasing piles of garbage. Also, they have been blamed for the decreasing runs of young steelhead and salmon that migrate to the sea and return to deposit and fertilize new eggs in their mountain-home streams.

Recently, while I was photographing gulls at Garibaldi, Oregon, a commercial fisherman told me, "I wish the whole race of gulls could be exterminated. The salmon and steelhead used to fill the streams in summer and winter runs. Now the gulls are so numerous they catch most of the young fry before they reach the sea."

This man apparently had never given a thought to how bad logging practices in the high mountain timber country had stripped the trees from the stream sides, destroyed gravel spawning beds, and allowed the sun to raise temperatures beyond the critical level for fish reproduction. Nor had he considered the man-made disaster brought by too many dams, too much industry, and too much thermal pollution that now threatens aquatic life by producing unnatural overbalances of harmful bacteria, algae, and fishes, unsuitable for sports fishing, that feed upon the natural stream food formerly available to game fish. Instead, he blamed the gulls.

Man has influenced gull populations in one way or another for more than a hundred years. Plume hunters of North America in the last century almost depleted the rocky islands of gulls and terns on the northeastern coast. Egg hunters and fishermen destroyed gull nests by the thousands so that they could return and gather fresh eggs when the gulls nested a second time. Not until the Migratory Bird Treaty Act between Canada and the

The freedom, beauty, and grace of gull flight are cause for fascination and inspiration.

United States was signed in 1916 did gulls and other sea birds get the protection that enabled them to reestablish their colonies.

Long before this, a law was passed in Utah to protect the state bird, the California gull. The story is often told about the gulls that saved the crops of the pioneers in 1848 by devouring the Mormon crickets that appeared in countless millions.* William H. Behle writes of these gulls that "stress has been placed upon their sudden arrival and the implication is that they made their appearance just for the crisis and had never before been seen." The gulls, however, had been associated with the Great Salt Lake area before the plague of crickets occurred. But they did save the crops and their effort is commemorated by the beautiful gull monument on the Temple Grounds in Salt Lake City.

Editor's Note: The Mormon "crickets" are western long-horned grasshoppers, *Anabrus simplex,* related to katydids. They are robust, clumsy-appearing insects with wings too short for flying.

Gulls and Men

Gulls have long been recognized in legend and folklore, and as omens of good fishing by their behavior over schools of bait fish that attract tuna. Gulls, and man-o'-war birds, or frigate-birds, have been regarded by sailors as forecasters of the weather. Many artists have painted gulls in seascapes; one of the most beautiful of these is "Seagulls" by the Swedish artist Bruno Liljefors. It is in the National Museum in Stockholm. The gull also appears on the 1 sen, 1938-1940 coin of Japan.

Thoughtless, or sometimes deliberate, acts of men kill many gulls and shore birds. Among the worst killers are oil slicks that form after ships pump out their bilges or after offshore oil wells spring leaks and send sticky goo onto the beaches, killing hundreds of birds. One of these disasters was the oil spill on the Santa Barbara, California, beach in 1969. More recently, oil spills have occurred in the Gulf of Mexico and along the Aleutian Islands.

Another man-made problem is that of helicopters flying close to bird rocks. The young birds are blown out of their nests or jump from the cliffs to their deaths on the rocks below. The Coast Guard cannot be blamed when they have to fly rescue missions for thoughtless people who should not climb the rocks in the first place. Even if the climbers need no rescue, they frighten the adult birds from their nests and some fail to return.

Gulls now are recognized as serious hazards at airports, where jet engines are liable to damage by birds sucked in at take-off. Large birds also give confusing echoes and images on radar screens. These hazards are often created by the establishment of airports near ponds and in former swamps or mud flats where water birds have lived for centuries.

A recent proposal that the city of Portland, Oregon, establish its garbage dump near the juncture of the Sandy and Columbia Rivers brought strong opposition because of the destruction of the area's beauty and because of the gulls that would congregate near the end of the runway at Troutdale Airport. Even now the gulls in flight dent the airplanes and create hazards for students who are training to be pilots.

A more subtle influence on fish-eating birds is now resulting from increases of DDT and other chemicals in the environment. The menace of chlorinated hydrocarbons has already been established for peregrine falcons and other raptors on both sides of the Atlantic. Recent pesticide research has indicated that eggshell thinning caused by DDE, a breakdown product of DDT, causes easily broken eggs, with shells almost nonexistent for brown pelicans on Anacapa Island off southern California. Sooty terns on the Dry Tortugas, off Florida, also produced thin-shelled eggs and only a fraction of the normal number of young.

Now, the shell thickness of herring gull eggs collected from five states has decreased with increases in chlorinated hydrocarbon residues. Joseph J. Hickey and Daniel W. Anderson found that clutch size decreased and embryonic mortality was high when DDE residues in eggs averaged 202 parts per million. These researchers conclude that "these persisting chemical compounds are having a serious insidious effect on certain species at the tops of contaminated ecosystems."

Conflicts between men and gulls take many other forms. In addition to eating berry, vegetable, and grain crops of farmers, gulls become involved with electrical companies, golfers, and sportsmen. George Laycock reported an instance of gulls dropping nuts and bolts on the skylights of a London factory in 1947. Apparently the gulls did not distinguish between these objects and the clams they are accustomed to dropping on rocks along the ocean shore.

Birds are electrocuted by transmission lines in all parts of the country. For a time gulls caused short circuits in the lines of the Carolina Power and Light Company. The problem was solved by spacing the wires farther apart than the wingspread of the gulls.

I have seen gulls pick up and fly away with golf balls at the Rose City Golf Course in Portland, Oregon. But this is nothing new. On November 20, 1930, Earle R. Greene watched a herring gull in Atlanta, Georgia, carry a golf ball from the green to a nearby lake. The gull dipped the ball in the water, apparently to soften it, but observers were unable to determine whether the ball was swallowed or dropped into the water.

Gulls and Men

Fishermen complain frequently about gulls. If fish catches are left unguarded in weirs, the gulls occasionally eat some of the catch. Gulls that perch on boats, wharves, and buildings sometimes become objectionable because of their excrement. Hog raisers in the East complain that gulls eat the feed intended for their swine. And fish offal used as fertilizer in fields is pilfered by gulls. Sportsmen sometimes object to the depredations of gulls on eggs and young of geese and ducks.

Many methods have been used to control gulls. At the Newark, New Jersey, airport, taped distress calls of herring and black-headed gulls

A watchful gull among the fishing boats at Garibaldi, Oregon.

scared off most of the birds. The squawks from loudspeakers mounted on moving automobiles made the gulls change their flight patterns. This method did not work in Europe, where stationary loudspeakers were used.

Problems caused by gulls around airports and in agricultural areas have risen because of the difficulty of getting laymen to apply the knowledge already available from biological field studies. Even government agencies are unwilling to plan in accordance with natural principles. Instead, they seek technological solutions—noise, guns, poisons—or ignore the cost of bird problems.

Control problems caused by ravens, crows, and gulls can be approached through biological management. Marsh management at the Bear River Migratory Bird Refuge in Utah, for example, has successfully reduced depredation where predators such as gulls raid up to one-third of the duck nests in sparse vegetation. Behavior studies of the function and needs of the important water birds have led to deliberate planting and management of marsh plants that provide dense cover for nesting birds.

Through protection many sea birds have been given a new lease on life. But some species, such as the great black-backed gull, have increased at the expense of the eider duck, other gulls, and terns. Even when this happens, control should not be undertaken blindly. Alfred O. Gross has emphasized that "it becomes a debatable question of how much control should be administered until we clearly understand the interrelations of all the species involved while their populations become adjusted and stabilized under new conditions created by man."

Numerous gull-control methods have been tried in the past. Niko Tinbergen (1967) tells us that herring gulls on the island of Terschelling are controlled by allowing the islanders to collect and cook the eggs over fires on the beach at the edge of the dunes. Collecting is allowed only in certain areas and the helpers pay a guilder for permission to indulge in this form of recreation.

Shooting gulls has never been an efficient method of control. More certain results are obtained by shaking the eggs and returning them to the nest. The gulls continue to incubate and do not lay a second set. A newer method, used in the United States, is to spray the eggs with an oil emulsion containing Formalin.

Poisoning and shooting adult birds, as well as spraying their eggs, do not deal directly with the biological cause of the gull's increased numbers: excess food available at garbage dumps, open sewers, and fish processing plants. When better disposal methods for industrial wastes and garbage are developed, much of the big handout of free rations for scavenging gulls will be eliminated.

On agricultural lands, away from the cities, gulls are generally accepted as beneficial birds. They frequent crop lands for insect food and at times have been instrumental in controlling plagues of mice and other small

Herring gulls at Cornucopia, Wisconsin, at the edge of Lake Superior.

Gulls and ships go together.

mammals. Many farmers also enjoy the aesthetic appearance of the gulls that follow their plows in the spring and hunt grasshoppers in their meadows in summer.

In cities, gulls are usually fearless like pigeons, occasionally accepting food from people. They patrol the rivers that flow through cities and are a part of the scene wherever boats and wharves are found. They work over beaches for the scraps left by picnickers. And always they attract interest because of their graceful flight and ability to ride with all the winds.

Individual gulls appear so regularly at certain places at the same time each day that many people come to accept them as personal pets. I have known several gulls that came to office windows each noon to be fed during the lunch hour. The one that regularly stood on a ledge outside my office

Gulls dive for food in the back yard of a friendly neighbor.

Gulls alight with wings uplifted and landing gear extended.

Gulls search for food placed on tables and bird feeders by friendly people.

window in Portland, Oregon, apparently equated human presence with the days of the week. When I went to the office on Saturday or Sunday the gull was not there. If he ever came on weekends he possibly sensed by the lack of activity in the building that food would not be forthcoming.

There are numerous reports of pet gulls. Lyle Kirk, of Oceanside, Oregon, used to feed a pet gull, Elmer, that took food from a white dish. Mr. Kirk knew him because a dog had caught him and injured a wing

Above: a study in gull facial expressions as the last of the food is gobbled.

Opposite page: camera studies of tame gulls reveal the dynamics of their flight and provide enriching memories.

which never folded completely. One day the gull came across the beach with a limp. The minister of the local church wondered if it was Elmer, and the gull came at once when Mr. Kirk waved his arm. Then Elmer was gone for several weeks and when he returned with a companion Mr. Kirk changed his name to Gertrude.

A herring gull kept in confinement from October until February in Massachusetts by E. O. Marshall provided opportunity for many observations of habits and food preferences. The gull was kept in a house with seven fowls and many human visitors. Both wings were wounded and the gull soaked them in a dishpan filled with water and then spent as much as two hours arranging his feathers.

He never interfered with the chickens but would permit no familiarity. He became confused when a light was brought near him at night. On moonlit nights he was aware of the sudden appearance of people at the window of his house. He preferred animal to vegetable food and especially enjoyed herring, half grown rats, and dead mice. He ate bread, cheese, and grease and preferred mashed buttered potatoes and turnips to whole ones. Finally, when his wings had healed and his choice foods had given out, he flew through the opened doorway on February 6 and vanished in the direction of the seacoast.

Francis Harper, in "Birds of the Ungava Peninsula," records some observations of a pair of herring gull chicks reared from the downy stage by John Macko, who cooked at a camp near the north end of Ashuanipi Lake. The young gulls were fed raw meat and fish, including minnows from the lake. They flew away about the middle of August but returned to camp several times each day to be fed. On August 30, when they were full grown but in immature plumage, they still swam to shore and took strips of fish from Macko's hands.

Opposite page: gulls follow the plow and other farm implements to obtain upturned insects and other small animals.

There is a report by Edward R. Warren of a kittiwake becoming a pet. Two birds three or four days old when captured in the Gulf of St. Lawrence fed freely on pieces of fish but would not drink. When one died the other was given salt water to drink. It grew rapidly, became beautiful, and could fly within a month. It never tried to escape and freely permitted handling and caressing.

When the kittiwake was taken to Professor Alpheus Hyatt's summer home in Annisquam, Massachusetts, it flew about the harbor but always returned to spend the night in the pail where it was raised. When it made its first flight, it soared swiftly with perfect ease but did not know how to alight. It tumbled against its keeper and fell to the ground. Several flights were necessary before it learned to land by itself. Eventually it flew away across the marshes and was never seen again.

Experiences like these tell us much about gull habits and food preferences. But scientific studies of many birds are necessary to pinpoint migration routes, population changes, and behavioral responses. For many years gulls have been favorite subjects for experiments and studies of their mental, physical, and colonial habits.

Gull populations have been studied extensively by counting birds in nesting colonies, by aerial censuses based on photographs taken from airplanes, and by the Audubon Society Christmas Bird Counts. From data of this kind John A. Kadlec has concluded that the herring gull breeding population of New England has been doubling every twelve to fifteen years since the early 1900's. This increase has resulted from establishment of new colonies and expansion of breeding range.

Kadlec states that over half a million herring gulls have been banded and about twenty thousand recoveries have been reported. He concludes that mortality rates based on band recoveries are too high to be consistent with the observed rate of population growth, productivity, and age structure of the population. Loss of bands increases the likelihood of error in such studies.

In an extensive study of gulls of the Pacific slope of North America, Angus M. Woodbury and Howard Knight used colored bands on 14,091 gulls. Of these, 639 were recovered and 364 sight records were reported by trained observers. The greatest range of geographic movement was exhibited by young California gulls, which fan out from the Great Basin toward the Pacific coast. They disperse along the coast from Vancouver, British Columbia, southward almost to the tip of Baja California. Western gulls banded at Three Arch Rocks and Haystack Rock off the coast of Oregon spread north and south along the coast. Of the young glaucous-winged gulls banded in the Puget Sound-Georgia Strait area, most remained near their breeding grounds but a few traveled long distances down the Pacific coast.

Answers to old questions about gull travels are also being obtained by ornamenting gull wings with colored dye. It is not unusual now to see red, yellow, green, and blue gulls along the Atlantic coast, in city garbage dumps, and in the vicinity of airports. The gulls are trapped with nets either on the nest or at garbage-disposal areas.

The question has been raised whether artificial coloring causes any social problems for a gull. I know of no specific experiments to answer this question, with the exception of a study by Neal Griffith Smith. He altered the mantle color of glaucous gulls and Thayer's gulls by spraying the entire mantle, except the wing tips, with black, gray, or white. The color seemed to have no signal value to the gulls; consequently, function of the mantle coloration remains unknown. Alterations in wing-tip patterns with paint did not affect copulatory behavior when the patterns were displayed by resting gulls. But the gulls did use wing-tip patterns in discriminating between species when pairs were being formed. Incidentally, the gulls spent long periods in the water in attempts to wash off the paint.

A more complicated type of gull study by Neal Griffith Smith (1967) dealt with eye-head contrast among four species of gulls common to the eastern Canadian Arctic. The large glaucous gull has white wing tips and the iris of its eye is yellow. The fleshy ring around the eye is even brighter yellow. The herring gull has a yellow iris and an orange eye-ring. Thayer's gull has a dark brown iris and a reddish purple eye-ring. The smallest, Kumlien's gull, has an iris that varies from yellow to dark brown. Its eye-ring is reddish purple.

Smith changed the color of the eye-rings of the different gulls and also altered their wing-tip patterns. All the fascinating details of these studies and their results cannot be listed here. But the investigation led to speculation about the effect of "imprinting" of young birds on their parents and the possibility that a female Kumlien's gull, for example, chooses a mate with eye-head contrast and wing tips like those of her parents.

Thayer's gulls with eye-rings painted yellow were chosen as mates by glaucous females. Other crosses were obtained between species of gulls and pair formation was avoided or was disrupted when eye-ring color was changed. Even when pairs were formed, a change in eye-ring color broke the pair or resulted in separation or "divorce." These and other findings by Smith form the basis for hypotheses and further experiments relating to isolating mechanisms among species, evolution of populations, and genetic development.

From an entirely different standpoint, Vance A. Tucker studied the flight speed and endurance of laughing gulls and common parakeets, a phase of bird physiology that has intrigued people for many years. It has long been known that even small birds fly for many hours and for hundreds of miles without stopping. But little has been known about their efficiency or power expenditures.

Tucker taught the parakeets and gulls to fly in a wind tunnel. After several weeks of training, the birds wore transparent masks from which a tube led to analyzing equipment designed to determine the rate of carbon dioxide exhaled to oxygen consumed during flight.

The laughing gulls flew in the wind tunnel at speeds between 15 and 29 miles per hour. Power expenditure remained between 50 and 60 calories per gram per hour. Minimum power consumption was attained at a speed of 19 miles per hour. At this speed the gulls consumed less than 0.6 percent of their body weight per hour.

The efficiency of gull flight shown by this experiment provides an explanation of how these birds are able to cover large distances in their daily search for food and in the long seasonal migrations made by such species as Franklin's gulls. Tucker points out that "a walking or running mammal expends 10 to 15 times more energy to cover a given distance than a bird of the same size does. It is no wonder that small mammals do not undertake long seasonal migrations. Some birds can even travel more economically than some machines. For example, a pigeon flies more economically than a light plane." Men, horses, and automobiles likewise are less economical with energy than pigeons and gulls.

Many gull studies made in the field are as informative as those made in the laboratory. It has long been known that, as stated earlier, many birds, including gulls, dispose of egg shells soon after their chicks have hatched. This removes an attraction for birds that eat young gulls, especially carrion crows and large gulls which cruise over other gull colonies.

In a study made near Ravenglass on the Irish Sea coast of Cumberland, England, Niko Tinbergen (1963) painted gull eggs white, used dummy shells of different colors, and tested shape response with real egg shells, halves of ping-pong balls, paper, and other materials.

Crows and herring gulls showed preferences for natural-colored eggs, and carried away more white and khaki shells than red, blue, black, or green ones. Real egg shells were removed from their nests by brooding gulls more frequently than cylindrical rings, angular pieces, flat cardboard or metal strips. The experiment also indicated that gulls learned the color of their eggs during incubation. Birds that sat on black eggs removed more black rings from their nests than birds that sat on green or khaki-colored eggs.

Among the classical experiments with gulls in the field are those of Niko Tinbergen (1967) on behavior of herring gull chicks. In studying pecking responses, he used many dummy models of gull heads and bills painted with different colors. He found that red had a stronger influence than any other color.

Other tests included bill-tip color, influence of head color, influence of presence or absence of a head on the dummy, and the influence of various shapes of heads. The many details of these experiments cannot be described here. But Tinbergen believed that pecking by young gull chicks is an instinctive response that is released by the pattern presented by the parents' bills and heads.

A similar study of feeding behavior of gull chicks by Jack P. Hailman (1969) involving both laughing gulls and herring gulls leads to the interesting conclusion that instincts are not fully present at birth; experience and learning are involved in the developing interactions between the birds and their environment. Hailman's studies of gull chick feeding patterns were made with painted cards, wooden dowels approximating the size of an adult gull's beak, and numerous head dummies of different shapes and painted to show various contrasts.

One interesting finding was the failure of laughing gull chicks to discriminate between models of their own parents and those of herring gulls. Chicks also preferred bill models projecting from above to those that came from below. This choice tended to make the chicks peck at the parents' bills instead of their legs. The broad psychological interpretation of these tests was that the shape of the model was less important during the gull chick's early perceptual experiences than it was when experience had conditioned the chick to more accurate pecking. Then a highly configural shape was preferred.

In contrast with these studies, numerous investigations have been directed toward the life history, ecology, and population trends of gulls. A fine example of a detailed study of this kind is the report on California gulls in the Great Salt Lake region by William H. Behle. In British Columbia the breeding ecology of the glaucous-winged gull has been studied in detail by Kees Vermeer. The dynamics of the New England herring gull population is covered in the report by John A. Kadlec and

Gulls and Men

William H. Drury. Reports from Finland, Germany, and England show that gull populations and habits have changed in Europe as well as in America.

A storm coming in from the sea is not complete without the gulls.

The majority of these reports ascribe the increa~~~~~ ~ull numbers to availability of garbage, sewage, and other environmental disturbances by man. As one might expect, anti-gull sentiment is building up in localities where the gulls are becoming a nuisance to everything, from game birds to berry crops to airplanes. We hope, too, that anti-garbage and anti-exploitation sentiment regarding the environment will also build up. If man's pollution and desecration of nature ever get under control, then the future of gulls will be assured.

We need gulls. We need them not only as natural scavengers and for their balancing effect on the environment, but for their grace and beauty and for the lift they give to the spirit. The "prairie doves," or Franklin's gulls, fluttering behind the farmer's plow, are buffers against the materialistic world we have created by cultivation of the land. The raucous cacophony of gull voices in a breeding colony on the offshore islands of the Pacific or the cliffs of Newfoundland is an antidote for the miasma and noise of the great cities. The storm coming in from the sea is incomplete without the screaming gulls whose voices are as much a part of the scene as the howling gale and the thundering surf.

Gull Genera and Species

THE COMMON and scientific names of North American gulls follow those listed in the *Check-list of North American Birds,* Fifth Edition, published by the American Ornithologists' Union in 1957. The names of gulls of other lands follow those listed by W. B. Alexander in *Birds of the Ocean.* Some breeding ground and migration data have been taken from Jonathan Dwight, *The Gulls (Laridae) of the World; Their Plumiages, Moults, Variations, Relationships and Distribution.* Neal Griffith Smith (1966) has been followed for changes in classification of some Arctic gulls, updating the *Check-list of North American Birds* (1957). A few common names, used in the older literature, are given in parentheses. Information on the breeding grounds and migrations of American gulls also can be found in the book by Chandler S. Robbins, Bertel Bruun, and Herbert S. Zim, *A Guide to Field Identification—Birds of North America*, and in the Peterson Field Guide series of bird books by Roger Tory Peterson. Gull distribution data have been somewhat generalized in the following list, since the details are too lengthy for this book. For more complete information the reader is referred to the A.O.U. *Check-list.* For even more up-to-date ranges, the reader should look through recent issues of *Audubon Field Notes*, the October (nesting seasons) issues. For ease of reference, the gulls have been listed in alphabetical order of their common names, instead of in the phylogenetic (relationship) order of the bird check lists.

129

The World of the Gull

Aden gull, *Larus hemprichi*. Breeds on southern islands in the Red Sea and along the shores of the Gulf of Aden. Wanders along the coasts of Arabia to India and East Africa.

Andean gull, *Larus serranus*. Breeds on Lake Titicaca and other high-altitude lakes in Chile and Peru. Migrates to Pacific coasts of Chile, Equador, and Peru.

Audouin's gull, *Larus audouinii*. Breeds on islands of Sardinia and Corsica and islands off the coast of Spain. Wanders locally in the Mediterranean Sea and to the coast of Syria.

Black-legged kittiwakes, Cape Thompson, Alaska. These little gulls spend most of their time roaming over the oceans. (Photo by John Q. Hines)

Black-headed gull, *Larus ridibundus* (Northern black-headed gull). Breeds from British Isles, Scandinavia, and central Europe to Turkestan, and ranges in winter to the coasts of France, northern Africa, and east to the Persian Gulf, India, China and southern Japan. A race that breeds in eastern Siberia reaches the coasts of China and Japan in winter. Accidental in Greenland, Labrador, Newfoundland, Massachusetts, New York, and Mexico. Anthony J. Erskine reports that this bird is being seen more and more frequently in eastern North America.

Black-legged kittiwake, *Rissa tridactyla* (Common kittiwake). Breeds in arctic and subarctic regions from Alaska to northern coast of Siberia; in North America eastward from Alaska to Labrador and Newfoundland. Wanders south in winter from Newfoundland to southern New Jersey and the Bermudas, and rarely to eastern Florida; on the Pacific Coast south to northwestern Baja California. It also wanders along the Atlantic coasts of Europe and Africa; to the Mediterranean, Caspian, and Black Seas; also to the coast of Japan.

Black-tailed gull, *Larus crassirostris* (Temminck's gull, Japanese gull). Breeds on islands and shores of Japan Sea. Migrates as far south as Hong Kong on the coast of China. Accidental in San Diego Bay, California.

Bonaparte's gull, *Larus philadelphia*. Breeds in Alaska and western Canada. Migrates along the western coast of the United States and Mexico. Wanders inland in the western states and eastward to Ohio, southeastern Quebec, and Massachusetts; also to the West Indies and to the Hawaiian Islands. Winters casually in the United States along the west coast and in the east from southern Ontario, New England, and south to central Florida.

Buller's gull, *Larus bulleri*. Breeds on inland lakes and rivers of South Island, New Zealand. Moves to the coast and adjacent islands in the non-breeding season. This small gull is a local species.

California gull, *Larus californicus*. Breeds on inland lakes from California, Utah, and Wyoming north to Great Slave Lake, Canada; breeds locally in northwestern Nevada, southeastern Oregon, eastern Idaho, cen-

Telephoto shot of Bonaparte's gull on southward migration over the Pacific Ocean.

tral Montana, and east-central North Dakota. Winters south and west to coasts of British Columbia, California, Mexico, and Guatemala. Has been observed in Hawaii. California gulls are summer residents and are casual in winter in Colorado.

Chinese black-headed gull, *Larus saundersi* (Saunder's gull). Breeds on lakes in northern China and Mongolia. Migrates in winter to coasts of Korea and China; occasionally seen in Japan and Formosa.

In winter in the Pacific Northwest, California gulls, ring-billed gulls, and other gulls live in peace with one another and gather food in the same areas.

Dusky gull, *Larus fuliginosus*. Breeds on the Galapagos Islands and wanders among these islands in the nonbreeding season. A local equatorial species that does not migrate north or south.

Franklin's gull, *Larus pipixcan*. An inland gull that breeds around lakes in the plains of the northern United States and southern Canada. It also breeds in central Oregon, northwestern Utah, and northwestern Iowa. Recently, nonbreeding birds have been very common in eastern Colorado. Migrates as far south as the coast of Chile and Patagonia; occasional in the West Indies, Hawaiian Islands, and Galapagos Islands. This gull also winters along the northern coast of the Gulf of Mexico from Texas to Louisiana.

Glaucous gull, *Larus hyperboreus*. Breeds north of the Arctic Circle, Alaska, Hudson Bay, Labrador, Iceland to Siberia. Winters south on Pacific coasts to Japan and California; occasional in many areas, including the Great Lakes, New England, Bermuda Islands, Mediterranean, Caspian, and Red Seas.

Glaucous-winged gull, *Larus glaucescens*. Breeds on Pacific coast from Washington to Alaska, the Aleutian Islands, and from Kamchatka to northeastern Siberia. Winters southward to Japan and to California and Baja California. Casual in eastern China; accidental in the Hawaiian Islands.

Gray gull, *Larus modestus*. Inhabits the coasts of Chile and Peru and breeds on coastal islands. Wanders north to the Gulf of Guayaquil.

Great black-backed gull, *Larus marinus*. Breeds in North America from Nova Scotia to Labrador; in Greenland and Iceland; from eastern Labrador, Quebec, and maritime provinces south along the Atlantic coast from Maine and Massachusetts to Island Bay, New York. Also breeds in northern British Isles, Scandinavia, and northern Russia. Winters as far south as Florida, Cuba, Canary Islands, west coast of Africa, and Mediterranean and inland seas of Europe.

Great black-headed gull, *Larus ichthyaetus* (Great hooded gull). Breeds along Caspian Sea, Aral Sea, and inland lakes of southeastern Russia and

Glaucous-winged gull sailing on the wind over the Strait of Juan de Fuca.

Great black-backed gull on nest in Nova Scotia. This is the largest gull in the world. (Photo by Dr. George K. Peck)

Great black-backed gull.

eastward to central Asia. Winters in Red Sea, eastern Mediterranean Sea, Persian Gulf, and along the shores of India.

Heermann's gull, *Larus heermanni*. Breeds on islands in Gulf of California and islands off the coast of Mexico. Migrates northward along the Pacific coast as far as southern British Columbia. The only North American gull that wanders northward after the nesting season. Winters from Oregon to Guatemala.

Herring gull, *Larus argentatus*. Breeds over a wide area in the northern hemisphere and winters from southern limits of breeding range throughout North America to Panama; and to northern and central Africa, Arabia, India, French Indochina, and the northern Philippines. For details of the subspecies ranges see the A.O.U. *Check-list of North American Birds*. Four geographic races have different breeding ranges. The European herring gull breeds on the coasts and islands of northern France, British Isles, Denmark, Scandinavia, eastward to the White Sea and northern Russia. In winter it wanders south to the Mediterranean Sea, northern coast of Africa, and to the Canary Islands. The Vega herring gull breeds along the northern Siberian coast and wanders south in winter to the Japan coast, central China, Formosa, and the Alaskan coast. The American herring gulls breed along the southern coast of Alaska and British Columbia, on inland lakes across Canada to Hudson Bay, Labrador, and Maine south to New Jersey, Maryland, and Virginia. In winter they travel along both North American coasts as far south as Bermuda, Cuba, Texas, Yucatán, and the Tres Marias Islands off the coast of Mexico. They also winter about the Great Lakes, and along the Mississippi River and its tributaries. Thayer's gull, formerly considered a subspecies of the herring gull, recently has been rated as a full species by Neal Griffith Smith.

Iceland gull, *Larus glaucoides*. Neal Griffith Smith (1966) notes that the common name of *Larus glaucoides* in the A.O.U. *Check-list* is "Iceland gull." This name is misleading since *glaucoides* has rarely, if ever, bred on Iceland. It does nest in Greenland. Smith and previous investigators consider Kumlien's gull (*Larus glaucoides kumlieni*) to be a subspecies of the

Herring gulls. (Photo by Dorothy B. Taylor)

Iceland gull. Kumlien's gull is restricted to the western populations nesting on Baffin Island, northwestern Quebec, and certain islands in the Hudson Strait. The A.O.U. *Check-list* (1957) lists the winter range of the Iceland gull to include the Atlantic coast from southern Labrador to New York and New Jersey; the Great Lakes area; Iceland, British Isles, northern France, Belgium, Holland, Heligoland, and the Baltic area.

Indian black-headed gull, *Larus brunnicephalus*. Breeds in central Asia, northern India, and southern Mongolia. Winters south to coasts of India, Ceylon, Baluchistan, Persia, and Arabia.

Ivory gull, *Pagophila eburnea*. Breeds far north of Arctic Circle; in Old World, on Spitzbergen, Nova Zembla, and islands along the Siberian coast; in New World, on northern Greenland, Baffin Island, Grinnell Island, and Melville Island. Winters over drift ice and pack ice on coasts of southern Greenland, Iceland, Norway, Finland, northern Russia, and southeastern Siberia. In winter, occurs in Iceland, Labrador, Alaska, and as far south as Maine, Massachusetts, New York, New Jersey, Wisconsin, northern France, and Lake Geneva in Switzerland. A very rare visitor in British Columbia near Penticton, Ontario, and southwestern Quebec.

Laughing gull, *Larus atricilla*. Breeds along the Atlantic coast from northern Nova Scotia to Florida, Louisiana, and Texas. Also on islands off northern Yucatán, northern Venezuela, the coasts of Sonora and Sinaloa, and the Salton Sea in southeastern California. Winters from Pacific coast of southern Mexico to Ecuador and northern Peru, and from North Carolina south to Columbia, Venezuela, Brazil, and the West Indies.

Lesser black-backed gull, *Larus fuscus*. Breeds around Baltic Sea, White Sea, Scandinavia, British Isles, France, and Iceland; accidental in Greenland, New York, and Maryland. Winters from British Isles to northwest coast of Africa, Mediterranean Sea, and south to Lake Nyasa, Somaliland, and east coast of India.

Little gull, *Larus minutus*. Breeds in northern Russia and Asia and south to the Baltic and North Seas. Ranges in winter to Japan, northern India, southern Russia, the Mediterranean Sea, England, Bermuda Islands, Mexico, Maine, New York, New Jersey, Pennsylvania, Ohio, Massachusetts, Ontario, and Saskatchewan. This is the smallest of the gulls, being less than 1 foot in length.

Magellan gull, *Gabianus scoresbi*. Breeds on islands near tip of South America, including Falklands, South Shetland, and islands near Cape Horn. Ranges from Tierra del Fuego north along the coast of Chile and along the coast of Argentina.

Mediterranean black-headed gull, *Larus melanocephalus* (Adriatic gull). Breeds around the Black and Aegean Seas. Winters from Mediterranean Sea to Spain, Portugal, and France. Occasionally reaches England, Germany, and Switzerland.

Mew gull, *Larus canus*. Includes three races: *canus* breeds in northern Europe, including British Isles, Scandinavia, and Russia, and winters south to the Mediterranean Sea, Persian Gulf, and Egypt, and is casual in western Greenland; *major* breeds in eastern Siberia and migrates south to the coasts of China, Japan, and Formosa; *brachyrhynchus* breeds in northern British Columbia, Yukon, Alaska, northern Saskatchewan, and on islands in the Arctic Ocean, and winters south to San Diego, California, and is accidental in Wyoming, Massachusetts, and Quebec.

Pacific gull, *Gabianus pacificus*. Breeds on islands and southern coast of Australia and on coast of Tasmania. In nonbreeding season, frequents the southern and eastern coasts of Australia north to Queensland. It also ascends Australian and Tasmanian rivers. E. Thomas Gilliard in *Living Birds of the World* puts the Pacific gull in the genus *Larus*.

Patagonian black-headed gull, *Larus maculipennis*. Breeds on the Falkland Islands, in Tierra del Fuego, and on islands off the coast of Patagonia. Migrates northward on Atlantic coast to southern Brazil and on Pacific coast to Peru.

Red-legged kittiwake, *Rissa brevirostris*. Breeds on Pribilof, western Aleutian, Commander, and other islands in the Bering Sea. Little is known about its winter range. Accidental in west-central Yukon and northwest Oregon.

Ring-billed gulls are smaller than California gulls and western gulls with which they associate. The black ring encircling the bill is a distinguishing characteristic.

Red Sea black-headed gull, *Larus leucophthalmus* (White-browed gull). Lives as a resident in the Gulf of Aden and southern half of the Red Sea. Sometimes wanders to Suez, Arabia, and Somali coast.

Ring-billed gull, *Larus delawarensis*. Breeds in western North America from south-central Oregon eastward across southern Canada and northern United States, also on northern shore of the Gulf of St. Lawrence, Lake Melville in Labrador, and Great Slave Lake in Canada. Winters from Vancouver Island, British Columbia, south through Oregon and along the Pacific coast to Mexico; in the interior of the United States around larger lakes and rivers and along the Gulf of Mexico from Texas to Florida and Cuba. From the prairie lakes some gulls go to the nearest water that remains unfrozen through winter; others merely go to the nearest garbage dumps.

Ross's gull, *Rhodostethia rosea*. Breeds in northern Siberia and arctic islands. Winter range unknown. In migration there is one record for west-central Greenland; in late summer and fall goes east to Melville Peninsula, Franz Joseph Land, and Bennet Island; also known in Bering Sea, Pribilof Islands, and western Alaska. Accidental in Norway, France, and England.

Sabine's gull, *Xema sabini*. Breeds throughout the arctic from North America to Asia, including Alaska, northern Canada, the west coast of Greenland, and Spitzbergen. Winters in Europe south to the North Sea and occasionally in France, Germany, Denmark, and Holland. Migrates along the Pacific coast of North and South America as far south as Peru and northern Chile. Seen occasionally in New York, Texas, Colorado, Wyoming, Arizona, Nebraska, and other inland states and in the Bermuda Islands.

Silver gull, *Larus novaehollandiae*. Breeds, depending on the race, along coasts and islands of southern Australia, Tasmania, New Caledonia, and northern New Zealand. Some are yearlong residents; others migrate to the east coast of Australia. The race *hartlaubi* breeds on the coast of South Africa and wanders north on both the Indian Ocean and Atlantic Ocean coasts.

Simeon gull, *Larus belcheri* (Belcher's gull). Breeds on coastal islands of Chile and Peru and wanders northward after the breeding season. It is resident on the Falkland Islands.

Slaty-backed gull, *Larus schistisagus.* Breeds on shores and islands of Sea of Okhotsk, Kamchatka, and eastern Siberia south through the Kuriles to Hokkaido, Japan; seen at Harrowby Bay, northwestern Mackenzie. Winters from Kamchatka to Honshu, coasts of Japan and China, and to Amoy and Formosa. Casual or accidental in the Aleutians, Pribilof Islands, and the coast of Alaska.

Slender-billed gull, *Larus genei.* Breeds from southern Spain eastward to the Persian Gulf and on the Black and Caspian Seas. Wanders throughout the Mediterranean Sea to the west coast of Africa and eastward as far as India.

Southern black-backed gull, *Larus dominicanus* (Antarctic black-backed gull). Breeds and lives in nonbreeding season on shores and islands of the southern oceans and the southern coasts of South America and Africa. Also resident in New Zealand but not in Australia.

Swallow-tailed gull, *Creagrus furcatus* (*Larus furcatus*, according to some authors). Breeds on Galapagos Islands and wanders among local islands. Also found at Malpelo Island in the Bay of Panama, and along the coast of Peru.

Thayer's gull, *Larus thayeri.* Formerly listed as a subspecies of the herring gull, now is rated as a full species by Neal Griffith Smith (1966). Thayer's gull is medium sized and has a dark mottled-brown iris and a reddish-purple eye-ring. It is restricted to the islands of the Canadian arctic archipelago and northwestern Greenland, where it nests almost exclusively on cliffs.

Western gull, *Larus occidentalis.* Breeds on islands off the coasts of Washington, Oregon, and California, and the Farallon Islands to Baja California and in the Gulf of California to Sonora. Winters along the Pacific coast of its breeding range south from Washington to west coast of Mexico and in the Gulf of California.

Silver gull of Australia and New Zealand. (Photo by E. Slater, C.S.I.R.O., Australia)

Yellow-legged gull, *Larus cachinnans*. Breeds from Adriatic Sea to Lake Baikal, Siberia. Winters from Japan, China, India, and coasts of Arabia to the Mediterranean and Red Seas.

Bibliography

Alexander, W. B. *Birds of the Ocean.* New York: G. P. Putnam's Sons, 1963.

Allen, A. A. (ed.). "The Sea Gull's Story." *Bird-Lore*, 32:71-83 (1930).

Allen, Durward L. "Seaside Freeloader." *Field and Stream*, 68:49, 76, 78, 80 (1964).

American Ornithologists' Union. *Check-list of North American Birds.* Baltimore: Lord Baltimore Press, Inc., 1957.

Austin, Oliver L., Sr. "The Migration of the Common Tern (*Sterna hirundo*) in the Western Hemisphere." *Bird-Banding*, 24:39-55 (1953).

————, and Oliver L. Austin, Jr. "Some Demographic Aspects of the Cape Cod Population of Common Terns (*Sterna hirundo*)." *Bird-Banding*, 27:55-56 (1956).

Bailey, Alfred M., and Robert J. Niedrach. *Birds of Colorado.* Denver: Denver Museum of Natural History, 1965.

Bartholomew, George A., Jr., and William R. Dawson. "Temperature Regulation in Young Pelicans, Herons, and Gulls." *Ecology*, 35:466-472 (1954).

Beaudette, F. R. "Aspergillosis and Parasitism in a Gull." *Bird-Banding*, 16:99-101 (1945).

Beer, C. G. "Laughing Gull Chicks: Recognition of Their Parents' Voices." *Science*, 166:1030-1032 (1969).

Beetz, Johan. "Notes on the Eider." *The Auk*, 33:286-292 (1916).

Behle, William H. *The Bird Life of Great Salt Lake.* Salt Lake City: University of Utah Press, 1958.

————, and Wayne A. Goates. "Breeding Biology of the California Gull." *The Condor*, 59:235-246 (1957).

Bent, Arthur Cleveland. *Life Histories of North American Gulls and Terns.* New York: Dover Publications, Inc., 1963.

Bolander, L. Ph., Jr. "A Robin Roost in Oakland, California." *The Condor*, 34:142-143 (1932).

Buckley, P. A. "Foot-paddling in Four American Gulls, with Comments on Its Possible Function and Stimulation." *Zeitschrift für Tierpsychologie*, 23:395-402 (1966).

Cooke, Wells W. *Distribution and Migration of North American Gulls and Their Allies*. U. S. Department of Agriculture, Bulletin 292:1-70, 1915.

Cottam, Clarence. "California Gulls Feeding on Midges." *The Condor*, 47:216 (1945).

———. "Gulls as Vegetarians." *The Condor*, 46:127-128 (1944).

———, and Cecil S. Williams. "Food and Habits of Some Birds Nesting on Islands in Great Salt Lake." *Wilson Bulletin*, 51:150-155 (1939).

Coulson, J. C., and E. White. "Observations on the Breeding of the Kittiwake." *Bird Study*, 5:74-83 (1958).

Crowell, Ethel M., and Sears Crowell. "The Displacement of Terns by Herring Gulls at the Weepecket Islands." *Bird-Banding*, 17:1-10 (1946).

Darling, Louis. *The Gull's Way*. New York: William Morrow and Company, 1965.

Davis, T. W. W. "The Breeding Distribution of the Great Black-backed Gull in England and Wales in 1956." *Bird Study*, 5:191-215 (1958).

Davis, W. A., and L. S. McClung. "Aspergillosis in Wild Herring Gulls." *Journal of Bacteriology*, 40:321-323 (1940).

Deusing, Murl. "The Herring Gulls of Hat Island, Wisconsin." *Wilson Bulletin*, 51:170-173 (1939).

Dickinson, L. E. "Utilities and Birds." *Audubon Magazine*, 59:54-55, 86-87 (1957).

DuMont, Philip A. "Relation of Franklin's Gull Colonies to Agriculture on the Great Plains." *Transactions North American Wildlife Conference*, 5:183-189 (1941).

Dwight, Jonathan. *The Gulls (Laridae) of the World; Their Plumages, Moults, Variations, Relationships and Distribution*. New York: Bulletin of the American Museum of Natural History. Volume LII, Article III, pp. 63-401, 1925.

Bibliography

Emlen, John T., Jr. "Juvenile Mortality in a Ring-billed Gull Colony."
Wilson Bulletin, 68:232-238 (1956).

Fänge, R., K. Schmidt-Nielsen, and H. Osaki. "The Salt Gland of the
Herring Gull." *Biology Bulletin*, 115:162-171 (1958).

Freuchen, Peter, and Finn Salomonsen. *The Arctic Year*. New York: G. P.
Putnam's Sons, 1958.

Frings, Hubert, Mable Frings, Beverly Cox, and Lorraine Peissner.
"Auditory and Visual Mechanisms in Food-finding Behavior of the
Herring Gull." *Wilson Bulletin*, 67:155-170 (1955).

Frings, Hubert, Mable Frings, Joseph Jumber, Rene-Guy Busnel, Jacques
Giban, and Philippe Gramet. "Reactions of American and French
Species of *Corvus* and *Larus* to Recorded Communication Signals
Tested Reciprocally." *Ecology* 39:126-131 (1958).

Gilliard, E. Thomas. *Living Birds of the World*. Garden City, N. Y.:
Doubleday & Company, Inc., 1958.

Greene, Earle R. "A Herring Gull Takes Up Golf." *Bird Lore*, 33:186
(1931).

Gross, Alfred O. "Gulls of Muskeget Island." *Bulletin Massachusetts
Audubon Society*, 32:43-47 (1948).

———. "The Laughing Gull on the Coast of Maine." *Bird-Banding*,
16:53-58 (1945).

Guiguet, C. J. "The Birds of British Columbia (5) Gulls, Terns, Jaegers,
and Skua." Handbook No. 13. *British Columbia Provincial Museum*,
Victoria, B. C. (1967).

Hailman, Jack P. "How an Instinct Is Learned." *Scientific American*,
221:98-106 (1969).

———. "Strange Gull (?) of the Galapagos." *Audubon Magazine*,
68:180-184 (1966).

Harper, Francis. "Birds of the Ungava Peninsula." University of Kansas,
Museum of Natural History, Miscellaneous Publication No. 17, pp.
1-171 (1958).

Harrington, Robert W., Jr. "Parasites of the Herring Gull *Larus argentatus smithsonianus*." *Bowdoin College Bulletin*, 6:14-18 (1939).

Herman, Carlton M., and Gordon Bolander. "Fungus Disease in a
Glaucous-winged gull." *The Condor*, 45:160-161 (1943).

Hickey, Joseph J., and Daniel W. Anderson. "Chlorinated Hydrocarbons and Eggshell Changes in Raptorial and Fish-eating Birds." *Science*, 162:271-273 (1968).

Hoffman, Ralph. *Birds of the Pacific States*. Boston: Houghton Mifflin Company, 1955.

Johnson, R. A. "Predation of Gulls in Murre Colonies." *The Wilson Bulletin*, 50:161-170 (1938).

Kadlec, John A., and William H. Drury. "Structure of the New England Herring Gull Population." *Ecology*, 49:644-676 (1968).

Kruuk, H. "Predators and Anti-predator Behaviour of the Black-headed Gull *(Larus ridibundus)." Behaviour Supplement*, 11:1-129 (1964).

Laycock, George. "The Feathered Bomber." *Field and Stream*, 69:35, 91-93 (1964).

Lissaman, P. B. S., and Carl A. Schollenberger. "Formation Flight of Birds." *Science*, 168:1003-1005 (1970).

Manning, T. H. "The Birds of Banks Island." *National Museum of Canada*, Bulletin No. 143, Ottawa (1956).

Marshall, E. O. "Long-wings." *Bird Lore*, 15:195-197 (1913).

Matthews, Geoffrey V. T. "An Investigation of Homing Ability in Two Species of Gulls." *Ibis*, 94:243-264 (1952).

Meinertzhagen, R. *Pirates and Predators*. London: Oliver & Boyd, 1959.

Meyerriecks, Andrew J., and Robert Meyerriecks. "Brown Pelican is Victim of Gull Piracy." *Natural History*, 74:32-35 (1965).

Mills, D. H. "Herring Gulls and Common Terns as Possible Predators of Lobster Larvae." *Journal of Fishery Research Board of Canada*, 14:729-730 (1957).

Moynihan, M. "California Gulls and Herring Gulls Breeding in the Same Colony." *The Auk*, 73:453-454 (1956).

———. "Notes on the Behavior of Some North American Gulls. I. Aerial Hostile Behavior." *Behaviour*, 10:126-178 (1956).

———. "Notes on the Behavior of Some North American Gulls. II. Non-aerial Hostile Behavior of Adults." *Behaviour*, 12:95-182 (1958).

———. "Notes on the Behavior of Some North American Gulls. III. Pairing Behavior." *Behaviour*, 13:112-130 (1958).

Mörzer Bruijns, M. F. "Gulls Which Are a Menace to Other Species—

the Herring Gull Problem in the Netherlands." Reprinted from VII *Bulletin of the International Commission for Bird Preservation,* pp. 103-107 (1958).

Murphy, Robert Cushman. *Oceanic Birds of South America.* Volume 2. New York: American Museum of Natural History, 1936.

Noble, G. K., and W. Wurm. "The Social Behavior of the Laughing Gull." *Annals New York Academy of Science,* 45:181-220 (1943).

Odin, Clyde R. "California Gull Predation on Waterfowl." *The Auk,* 74:185-202 (1957).

————. "The Effect of Predation by California Gulls (*Larus californicus*) on Waterfowl Production." M.S. thesis, *Utah State Agricultural College,* 1951.

Palmer, Ralph S. "Lake Erie Niche for Gulls." *Natural History,* 73:48-51 (1964).

Peterson, Roger Tory. Peterson Field Guide Series. Boston: Houghton Mifflin Company.

Pettingill, Olin Sewall, Jr. "An 'Ancient' Herring Gull." *Eastern Bird-Banding News,* 30:180 (1967).

Pough, Richard H. *Audubon Water Bird Guide.* Garden City, New York: Doubleday, 1951.

Poulding, R. H. "Loss of Rings by Marked Herring Gulls." *Bird-Study,* 1:37-40 (1954).

Robbins, Chandler S., Bertel Bruun, and Herbert S. Zim. *A Guide to Field Identification—Birds of North America.* New York: Golden Press, 1966.

Smith, Neal Griffith. "Evolution of Some Arctic Gulls (*Larus*): An Experimental Study of Isolating Mechanisms." *Ornithological Monographs* No. 4, American Ornithologists' Union (1966).

————. "Visual Isolation in Gulls." *Scientific American,* 217:94-102 (1967).

Snyder, L. Ly. *Arctic Birds of Canada.* Toronto: University of Toronto Press, 1957.

Spärck, R. "The Food of the North European Gulls." *Proceedings Xth International Ornithological Congress,* Uppsala, pp. 588-591.

Sprunt, Alexander, Jr. "Tern Colonies of the Dry Tortugas Fort Jefferson

National Monument—1948." *Florida Naturalist*, 22:9-16 (1948).

Terres, John K. *Flashing Wings*. Garden City, New York: Doubleday, 1968.

Thiessen, G. J., and E. A. G. Shaw. "Acoustic Irritation of Ringbilled Gulls." *Journal of the Acoustical Society of America*, 29:1307-1309 (1957).

Tinbergen, Niko. "The Evolution of Behavior in Gulls." *Scientific American*, 203:118-130 (1960).

———. *The Herring Gull's World*. (Anchor Books edition) Garden City, New York: Doubleday & Company, Inc., 1967.

———. "The Shell Menace." *Natural History*, 72:28-35 (1963).

———, and A. C. Perdeck. "On the Stimulus Situation Releasing the Begging Response in the Newly Hatched Herring Gull Chick (*Larus a. argentatus* Pontopp.)." *Behaviour*, 3:1-38 (1950).

Tucker, Vance A. "The Energetics of Bird Flight." *Scientific American*, 220:70-78 (1969).

Twomey, Arthur C. "California Gulls and Exotic Eggs." *The Condor*, 50:97-100 (1948).

Vermeer, Kees. "The Breeding Ecology of the Glaucous-winged Gull (*Larus glaucescens*) on Mandarte Island, B. C." Occasional Papers of the *British Columbia Provincial Museum* No. 13 (1963).

Warren, Edward R. "A Pet Kittiwake." *Bird-Lore*, 29:243-246 (1927).

Weidmann, U. "Observations and Experiments on Egg-laying in the Black-headed Gull (*Larus ridibundus* L.)." *British Journal of Animal Behaviour*, 4:150-161 (1956).

Woodbury, Angus M., and Howard Knight. "Results of the Pacific Gull Color-banding Project." *The Condor*, 53:57-77 (1951).

York, G. T. "Grasshopper Population Reduced by Gulls." *Journal of Economic Entomology*, 42:837-838 (1949).

Index

Italic page numbers indicate illustrations.